16th Edition

Aerofilms Guide

FOOTBALL GROUNDS

Fully Revised for the **2008/2009** Season and featuring every
Barclays Premier League and Coca-Cola League Club

Ian Allan

PUBLISHING

16th Edition

Aerofilms Guide

FOOTBALL GROUNDS

Fully Revised for the **2008/2009** Season and featuring every
Barclays Premier League and Coca-Cola League Club

CONTENTS

Front cover: Manchester United's Old Trafford remains by far the largest League ground in England and, in the 50th anniversary year of the Munich disaster, it was also to be the destination of both the Premier League title and the Champions League trophy.
Back cover: Watford Vicarage Road.
Preceding pages: Crewe Alexandra, Gresty Road.

First published in 1993;
Reprinted 1993 (twice); Second edition 1994; Third edition 1995; Fourth edition 1996; Fifth edition 1997; Sixth edition 1998; Seventh edition 1999; Eighth edition 2000; Ninth edition 2001; tenth edition 2002; 11th edition 2003, reprinted 2003. 12th edition 2004; 13th edition 2005; 14th Edition 2006; 15th Edition 2007; 16th Edition 2008

ISBN 978 0 7110 3333 7

Published by Ian Allan Publishing
an imprint of Ian Allan Publishing Ltd, Hersham, Surrey KT12 4RG.
Printed in England by Ian Allan Printing Ltd, Hersham, Surrey KT12 4RG

Code: 0808/E2

INTRODUCTION

Welcome to the 16th edition of *Aerofilms Guide: Football Grounds*. As with the previous editions, we have endeavoured to update the book to reflect all of the latest changes to Premier and Football League grounds since the publication of the last edition 12 months ago.

For the new season, there are two entirely new grounds to record. Firstly, after several years of trying to relocate from its confined ground at Layer Road, Colchester United has finally managed to relocate to its new all-seater stadium on the A12. Of the 92 clubs that comprise the top four divisions in English football, almost one third have now moved grounds over the past 20 years and the pace of relocation seems to be almost accelerating as new grounds are either under construction or proposed for almost a further 10 teams. The second new stadium is not a new ground as such – the Don Valley Stadium in Sheffield was constructed in the 1990s – but sees football for the first time in the 2008/09 season with the enforced move of Rotherham United from its home of 101 years as a result of the club's new owners being unable to agree terms with Millmoor's owners.

Coming up from the Blue Star Premier League are clubs where both grounds have played host to League football in the past. The more straightforward is the 'other' St James' Park – the home of Exeter City – which again becomes a League venue after an absence of some five years. The second is Aldershot's Recreation Ground; Aldershot played at the ground until the club folded during the 1991/92 season. After a number of years progressing through the non-league pyramid, Aldershot Town restored League football to this Hampshire town after a gap of almost two

decades. Promotion from the top-flight of non-league football for two clubs means relegation for two others and, at the end of the 2007/08 season, Wrexham and Mansfield Town both failed to survive.

As always the editorial team hopes that you will have an enjoyable season and that your particular team achieves the success that you, as fans, think that it deserves. We trust that, whatever the season ultimately holds for your team, that you will make the most of the opportunities that the season has to offer.

We also hope that you will find this guide of use. As always, please e-mail any comments or corrections to the editor at: info@ianallanpublishing.co.uk

Disabled Facilities

We endeavour to list the facilities for disabled spectators at each ground. Readers will appreciate that these facilities can vary in number and quality and that, for most clubs, pre-booking is essential. Some clubs also have dedicated parking for disabled spectators; this again should be pre-booked if available.

Blom Aerofilms Ltd

Blom Aerofilms Limited have been specialists in aerial photography since 1919. Their library of aerial photographs, both new and old, is in excess of 1.5 million images. Aerofilms undertake to commission oblique and vertical survey aerial photography, which is processed and printed in their specialised photographic laboratory. Digital photomaps are prepared using precision scanners.

wembley

Wembley Stadium, Wembley National Stadium Ltd, Empire Way, London HA9 0DS

website: **WWW.WEMBLEYSTADIUM.COM**   tel no: **020 8795 5050**

Fax: 020 8795 5050

Brief History: Inaugurated for the FA Cup Final of 1923, and venue for many national and international matches including the World cup Final of 1966. Also traditionally used for other major sporting events and as a venue for rock concerts and other entertainments. Last used as a football ground for a World Cup qualifier against West Germany in October 2001. The original Wembley with its twin towers was demolished in 2002 when work started on the construction of the new ground. After some delay, the new Wembley was completed in the spring of 2007 with its first major match being the FA Cup Final in May 2007. Record attendance at original Wembley: 126,047; at rebuilt ground: 89,826

(Total) Current Capacity: 90,000 (all-seated)

Visiting Supporters' Allocation: not applicable

Nearest Railway Station: Wembley complex (Network Rail), Wembley Central (Network Rail and London Underground) and Wembley Park (London Underground)

Parking (Car): Very limited at the ground with residents' only schemes in adjacent housing areas.

Parking (Coach/Bus): As directed

Police Force: Metropolitan

Disabled Visitors' Facilities:

Wheelchairs: 310 spaces for wheelchair-bound fans throughout the ground; *Blind*: to be confirmed

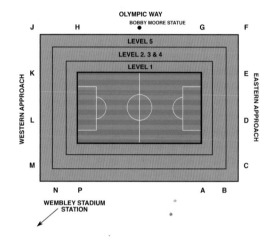

1 Olympic Way
2 Statue of Bobby Moore
3 To Wembley Park station
4 Wembley Complex
   railway station
5 To London Marylebone
6 To Wembley Central
7 Eastern Approach
8 Turnstiles 'G'
9 Turnstiles 'H'
10 Turnstiles 'F'
11 Turnstiles 'E'
12 Turnstiles 'D'

↑ *North direction (approx)*

◄ 700883
▼ 700884

1 A680 Whalley Road
2 To town centre and
   Accrington BR station (one
   mile)
3 Livingstone Road
4 Cleveleys Road
5 Coppice Terrace (away)

↑ North direction (approx)

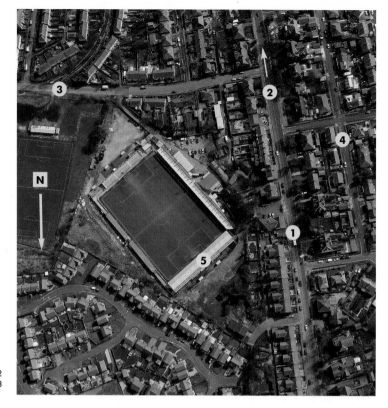

▸ 700962
▾ 700968

accrington stanley

Fraser Eagle Stadium, Livingstone Road, Accrington, Lancashire BB5 5BX

website: **WWW.ACCRINGTONSTANLEY.CO.UK**
e:mail: **INFO@ACCRINGTONSTANLEY.CO.UK**
tel no: **01254 356950**
colours: **WHITE SHIRTS, WHITE SHORTS**
nickname: **THE REDS, STANLEY**
season 2008/09: **LEAGUE TWO**

Accrington Stanley's second season back in the Football League proved slightly more successful than the first as John Coleman's team progressed to the heights of 17th position although there were concerns that the team might have got drawn into the relegation battle as both Wrexham and Mansfield started to pick up points late in the campaign. In the event, however, Stanley managed to beat the previous year's total of points by one; at this rate of progress the team will be challenging for the Play-Offs in about 30 years time! With one of the smallest grounds in the Football League, it's hard to escape the conclusion that Stanley may well face another fight in 2008/09 to preserve the club's hard-won League status.

Advance Tickets Tel No: 01254 356950
Fax: 01254 356951
Training Ground: New facility being sought for the 2007/08 season
Brief History: The original club was formed as Accrington Villa in 1891, becoming Accrington Stanley in 1895. The team entered the Football League in 1921 and remained a member until its resignation in 1962. Following four years outside the League, the original club folded in 1966 and was not resurrected until 1968. The club has been based at the Crown Ground (now called the Fraser Eagle stadium) since it was reformed but prior to 1966 the original club played at Peel Park, which is now demolished. Record Attendance (at Fraser Eagle Stadium) 4,368
(Total) Current Capacity: 5,057 (1,200 seated)
Visiting Supporters' Allocation: 400-1,500 max (in Coppice Terrace – covered)
Club Colours: Red shirts and white shorts
Nearest Railway Station: Accrington (20min walk)
Parking (Car): Free places at ground located behind both goals; on-street parking in vicinity of ground
Parking (Coach/Bus): As directed
Police Force and Tel No: Lancashire Police (01254 382141)
Disabled Visitors' Facilities:
Wheelchairs: Available. *Blind*: No special facility
Anticipated Development(s): A new cover was installed over the uncovered Coppice Terrace in late 2007.

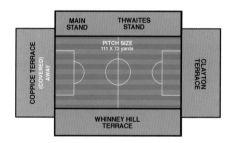

season 07/08: League Two **17TH** p46 w16 d3 l27 g/49 ga83

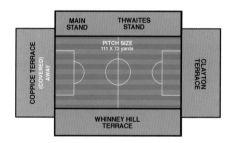

ACCRINGTON STANLEY F.C.

RESIGNED FROM THE FOOTBALL LEAGUE 1962

THE LONG ROAD BACK

RESURRECTION STARTED 1968

RETURNED TO THE FOOTBALL LEAGUE 2006

PRESENTED BY THOMAS & MATTHEW HAWORTH

aldershot town

Recreation Ground, High Street, Aldershot, Hampshire GU11 1TW

website: **WWW.THE SHOTS.CO.UK**
e:mail: **ACCOUNTS@THESHOTS.CO.UK**
tel no: **01252 320211**
colours: **RED SHIRTS, RED SHORTS**
nickname: **THE SHOTS**
season 2008/09: **LEAGUE TWO**

season 07/08: Blue Star Premier League **1ST** (promoted) p**46**; w**31**; d**8**; l**7**; gf**82**; ga**48**

Having missed out on restoring League football to this Hampshire town at the end of the 2003/04 season, when the club was defeated by Shrewsbury Town in the Play-Off final at the Britannia Ground, the team was to be one of two – the other being relegated Torquay United – that was to dominate the Blue Star Premier League in 2007/08. As the Devonian team's challenge faltered, Aldershot's promotion to the Football League was assured restoring League status to the Recreation Ground – albeit not to the old club as the original club folded in the early 1990s – after a gap of more than 15 years. Having amassed an impressive 101 points during the League season – 15 more than ultimate

runners-up Cambridge United – Gary Waddock's team should certainly have the potential to prosper at League Two level and a top-half finish is certainly a possibility.

Advance Tickets Tel No: 01252 320211
Fax: 01252 324347
Training Ground: Address withheld as it's located on MoD property
Brief History: Aldershot FC established in 1926 and played its first game at the Recreation Ground in 1927. Elected to the Football League (Third Division [South]) for the start of the 1932/33 season. Club failed to complete the 1991/92 season and lost its League membership. A new club, Aldershot Town, was established and, having progressed up the non-league pyramid, won promotion back to the Football League at the end of the 2007/08 season. Record attendance: (as Aldershot) 19,138; (as Aldershot Town) 7,500.
(Total) Current Capacity: 7,500 (1,885 seated)
Visiting Supporters' Allocation: c750 (243 seated) in the South Stand and East Bank.
Nearest Railway Station: Aldershot
Parking (Car): Pay & display car parks in the town centre
Parking (Coach/Bus): As directed
Police Force and Tel No: Hampshire (01962 841534)
Disabled Visitors' Facilities:
Wheelchairs:
Blind:

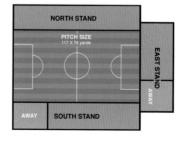

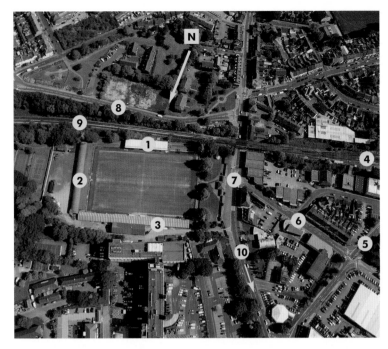

1 South Stand
2 East Bank
3 North Stand
4 Aldershot railway station
5 Windsor Way
6 Victoria Road
7 A323 High Street
8 Redan Road
9 Railway line towards Woking
   and London
10 A323 towards Fleet

↑ *North direction (approx)*

◂ 701172
▾ 701171

1 North Bridge
2 South Bridge
3 Drayton Park Station
4 Drayton Park
5 East Coast Main Line
6 To Finsbury Park Station
7 To Arsenal
   Underground Station
8 South East Corner (away)

↑ North direction (approx)

arsenal

Emirates Stadium, Highbury House, 75 Drayton Park, London N5 1BU

website: **WWW.ARSENAL.COM**
e:mail: **INFO@ARSENAL.CO.UK**
tel no: **020 7704 4000**
colours: **RED AND WHITE SHIRTS, WHITE SHORTS**
nickname: **THE GUNNERS**
season 2008/09: **PREMIER LEAGUE**

season 07/08: Premier League **3RD** p**38** w**24** d**11** l**3** gf**74** ga**31**

In the club's first season since the departure of Thierry Henry, the Gunners had a curate's egg of a season depending on which team turned up to play (even more confusingly the same players were largely involved in both!). At times – such as in the defeat of AC Milan in the San Siro Stadium in the Champions League – the team could play some dazzling football; on other occasions, such as the FA Cup defeat at Old Trafford, the team never really seemed to get going. For the first half of the League season, Arsenal seemed to be running away with the title as a significant points gap grew up between Chelsea, with their stuttering start to the season, and Manchester United, but come the New Year, Arsenal were overtaken by both ultimately to finish in third position. Over the years, Arsene Wenger has proved remarkably reluctant to spend heavily, preferring to see youngsters come through, but with a significant amount of money available – even after the costs of constructing the new stadium – Wenger may well be forced to break a habit of a lifetime, particularly if, as seems likely, a number of his top players are tempted away from the Emirates Stadium. Undoubtedly Arsenal will again be a major challenger for domestic and European silverware, but how serious they are as contenders will depend fundamentally on how much of his undoubtedly talented squad Wenger can retain and on the quality of those new faces that he brings in.

Advance Tickets Tel No: 020 7704 4040
Fax: 020 7704 4001
Training Ground: Bell Lane, London Colney, St Albans AL2 1DR
Brief History: Founded 1886 as Royal Arsenal, changed to Woolwich Arsenal in 1891 and Arsenal in 1914. Former grounds: Plumstead Common, Sportsman Ground, Manor Ground (twice), moved to Arsenal Stadium in 1913 and to new Emirates Stadium for start of the 2006/07 season. Record attendance (at Highbury) 73,295; 60,161 (at Emirates Stadium)
(Total) Current Capacity: 60,432
Visiting Supporters' Allocation: 3,000 (South East Corner)
Club Colours: Red and white shirts, white shorts
Nearest Railway Station: Finsbury Park or Drayton Park (Network Rail); Arsenal and Holloway Road (Underground)
Parking (Car): Residents' only parking scheme with special permits in the streets surrounding the ground and local road closures on matchdays
Parking (Coach/Bus): Queensland Road and Sobell Centre car park or as directed by the police
Police Force and Tel No: Metropolitan (020 7263 9090)
Disabled Visitors' Facilities:
Wheelchairs: c250 places around the ground
Blind: tbc
Anticipated Development(s): The club moved into the new Emirates Stadium for the start of the 2006/07 season, leaving Highbury, its home for the past 93 years, to be redeveloped as apartments although the work will incorporate the listed structures at the ground.

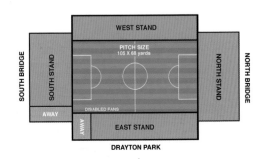

aston villa

Villa Park, Trinity Road, Birmingham, B6 6HE

website: **WWW.AVFC.PREMIUMTV.CO.UK**
e:mail: **ENQUIRIES@BUSINESSVILLA.CO.UK**
tel no: **0121 327 2299**
colours: **CLARET AND BLUE SHIRTS, WHITE SHORTS**
nickname: **THE VILLANS**
season 2008/09: **PREMIER LEAGUE**

A season of considerable promise for Martin O'Neill's team saw Villa challenging for a UEFA spot right up until the final Sunday of the season. Although results on the last day – Everton's comprehensive victory over Newcastle United allied to Villa's draw away at West Ham – meant that the all-important fifth place in the Premier League went to Merseyside, the rise of several young players such as Gabriel Agbonlahor potentially bodes well for the future. However, much will depend on the club's ability to hold on to the more influential members of the squad with the likelihood that Gareth Barry for one will be plying his trade elsewhere in 2008/09. Villa should certainly have the potential to compete next season for a position at the top of the also-rans but the dominance of the 'Big Four' means it's unlikely that the club can better fifth or sixth position.

Advance Tickets Tel No: 0800 612 0970
Fax: 0121 322 2107
League: F.A. Premier
Training Ground: Bodymoor Heath Lane, Middleton, Tamworth B78 2BB
Brief History: Founded in 1874. Founder Members Football League (1888). Former Grounds: Aston Park and Lower Aston Grounds and Perry Barr, moved to Villa Park (a development of the Lower Aston Grounds) in 1897. Record attendance 76,588
(Total) Current Capacity: 42,640 (all seated)
Visiting Supporters' Allocation: Approx 3,000 in Doug Ellis Stand
Nearest Railway Station: Witton
Parking (Car): Asda car park, Aston Hall Road
Parking (Coach/Bus): Asda car park, Aston Hall Road (special coach park for visiting supporters situated in Witton Lane)
Police Force and Tel No: West Midlands (0121 322 6010)
Disabled Visitors' Facilities:
Wheelchairs: Trinity Road Stand section
Blind: Commentary by arrangement
Anticipated Development(s): In order to increase the ground's capacity to 51,000 Planning Permission has been obtained to extend the North Stand with two corner in-fills. There is, however, no confirmed timescale for the work to be completed.

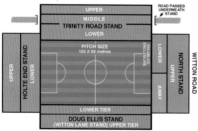

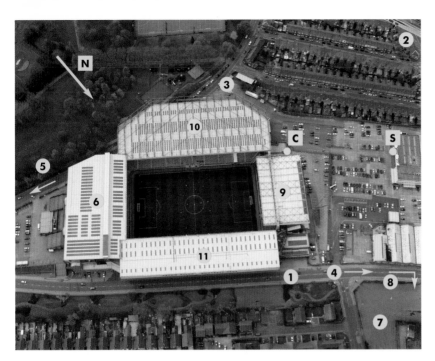

C Club Offices
S Club Shop

1 B4137 Witton Lane
2 B4140 Witton Road
3 Trinity Road
4 To A4040 Aston Lane to A34
  Walsall Road
5 To Aston Expressway & M6
6 Holte End
7 Visitors' Car Park
8 Witton railway station
9 North Stand
10 Trinity Road Stand
11 Doug Ellis Stand

⬆ North direction (approx)

◀ 701001
▼ 701003

C Club Offices
S Club Shop

1 Barnet Lane
2 Westcombe Drive
3 A1000 Barnet Hill
4 New Barnet BR station
(one mile)
5 To High Barnet tube station,
M1 and M25
6 South Stand

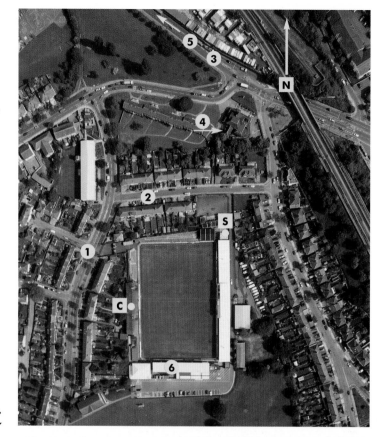

701191 ▶
701197 ▼

barnet

Underhill Stadium, Barnet Lane, Barnet,Herts EN5 2DN

website: **WWW.BARNETFC.PREMIUMTV.CO.UK**
e:mail: **INFO@BARNETFC.COM**
tel no: **020 8441 6932**
colours: **BLACK/GOLD SHIRTS, BLACK SHORTS**
nickname: **THE BEES**
season 2008/09: **LEAGUE TWO**

Under Paul Fairclough, the Bees enjoyed a season of further League Two consolidation, improving slightly on the position achieved at the end of the 2006/07 season. Outside the League, the club also achieved some modest success, most notably a 2-1 home victory over League One strugglers Gillingham in the 1st round of the FA Cup and a victory on penalties over another League One side – Swindon Town – in a 3rd round replay following a draw at the County Ground. For the new season, having achieved a top-half – just – finish in 2007/08, the team ought to have the potential to build upon this in the new season although a Play-Off place may be beyond the team's capabilities.

Advance Tickets Tel No: 020 8449 6325
Fax: 020 8447 0655
Brief History: Founded 1888 as Barnet Alston. Changed name to Barnet (1919). Former grounds: Queens Road and Totteridge Lane; moved to Underhill in 1906. Promoted to Football League 1991; relegated to Conference 2001; promoted to League 2 2005. Record attendance, 11,026
Total) Current Capacity: 5,500
Visiting Supporters' Allocation: 1,000 on East Terrace plus 500 on North Terrace if required.
Nearest Railway Station: New Barnet (High Barnet – Tube)
Parking (Car): Street Parking and High Barnet station
Parking (Coach/Bus): As directed by police
Other Clubs sharing ground: Arsenal Reserves
Police Force and Tel No: Metropolitan (020 8200 2112)
Anticipated Development(s): Following the granting of Planning Permission, the club opened its new £500,000 1,000-seat South Stand on 22 January 2008. The 200 seats from the uncovered temporary stand have been relocated under cover at the northeast side of the ground for use by away fans.

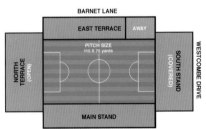

BARNET LANE

EAST TERRACE   AWAY

PITCH SIZE
115 X 75 yards

NORTH TERRACE (OPEN)

SOUTH STAND (COVERED)

WESTCOMBE DRIVE

MAIN STAND

PRIORY GROVE / FAIRFIELD WAY

barnsley

Oakwell Stadium, Grove Street, Barnsley, S71 1ET

website: **WWW.BARNSLEYFC.PREMIUMTV.CO.UK**
e:mail: **THERED@BARNSLEYFC.CO.UK**
tel no: **01226 211211**
colours: **RED SHIRTS, WHITE SHORTS**
nickname: **THE TYKES**
season 2008/09: **CHAMPIONSHIP**

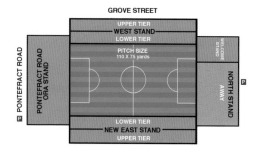

Towards the end of the season it looked as though Barnsley was going to achieve a remarkable double: an appearance in an FA Cup Final for the first time since World War 1 allied to relegation from the League Championship. In the event, neither was to happen although it was a close run thing in both cases for Simon Davey's team. In the FA Cup victory away at Liverpool in the 5th round set up a home quarter final against Chelsea. A further victory here, 1-0, saw the Tykes head to the new Wembley for the semi-final; unfortunately defeat by Cardiff City meant that a return visit to Wembley was ruled out. Without the distraction of the cup run, the team strung together a number of creditable performances in the League although a final day 3-0 reverse – ironically again against Cardiff – meant that the team ultimately finished only three points off the drop zone. For 2008/09 the Championship looks likely to be even tighter with potentially strong teams, such as Nottingham Forest being promoted, and so the Tykes could again face a struggle to maintain their Championship status.

Advance Tickets Tel No: 0871 226 6777

Fax: 01226 211444

Training Ground: Adjacent to ground

Brief History: Founded in 1887 as Barnsley St Peter's, changed name to Barnsley in 1897. Former Ground: Doncaster Road, Worsboro Bridge until 1888. Record attendance 40,255

Total Current Capacity: 23,009

Visiting Supporters' Allocation: 6,000 maximum (all seated; North Stand)

Nearest Railway Station: Barnsley

Parking (Car): Queen's Ground car park

Parking (Coach/Bus): Queen's Ground car park

Police Force and Tel No: South Yorkshire (01266 206161)

Disabled Visitors' Facilities:
Wheelchairs: Purpose built disabled stand
Blind: Commentary available

Future Development(s): With the completion of the new North Stand with its 6,000 capacity, the next phase for the redevelopment of Oakwell will feature the old West Stand with its remaining open seating. There is, however, no timescale for this work.

C Club Offices
S Club Shop
E Entrance(s) for visiting
  supporters

1 A628 Pontefract Road
2 To Barnsley Exchange BR
  station and M1 Junction 37
  (two miles)
3 Queen's Ground Car Park
4 North Stand
5 Grove Street
6 To Town Centre

↑ North direction (approx)

◄ 701015
▼ 701021

▲ 701032
▶ 701034

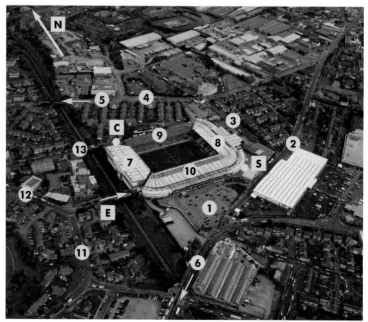

C Club Offices
S Club Shop
E Entrance(s) for visiting
supporters

1 Car Park
2 B4128 Cattell Road
3 Tilton Road
4 Garrison Lane
5 To A4540 & A38 (M)
6 To City Centre and
New Street BR Station
(1½ miles)
7 Railway End
8 Tilton Road End
9 Main Stand
10 Kop Stand
11 Emmeline Street
12 Kingston Road
13 St Andrew's Street

↑ *North direction (approx)*

birmingham city

St Andrew's Stadium, St Andrew's Street, Birmingham B9 4NH

website: **WWW.BCFC.PREMIUMTV.CO.UK**
e:mail: **RECEPTION@BCFC.COM**
tel no: **0844 557 1875**
colours: **BLUE AND WHITE SHIRTS, WHITE, SHORTS**
nickname: **THE BLUES**
season 2008/09: **CHAMPIONSHIP**

With uncertainty over his long-term future at the club as a result of an on-off take-over of the club (which ultimately failed to proceed), Steve Bruce, despite having guided the club back into the Premier League at the end of the 2006/07 season, resigned as manager at the end of November. Following a brief dispute over the termination of his contract, he was installed as new manager at Wigan. The club acted swiftly in appointing ex-Scotland boss, Alex McLeish – who had come close to securing Scotland's qualification for the Euro 2008 championship – as the new manager. Whilst the club seemed to spend much of the season thereafter hovering just above the drop zone, as Bolton and Fulham both improved their position, City was dragged back into the relegation mire. Crucial results were the 2-2 draw with Liverpool at St Andrews – when City had been 2-0 up – and the 2-0 defeat away at fellow strugglers Fulham in the penultimate game of the season. This left McLeish's team rooted in the bottom two and reliant on results elsewhere to ensure Premier League survival. In the event, despite a comprehensive 4-1 victory over Blackburn in a match that featured perhaps the miss of the season, results elsewhere consigned City to an immediate return to the Championship. Away from the League, City suffered a 2-1 defeat away at League One outfit Huddersfield Town in the third round of the FA Cup. As a relegated team, with the security of the two-year parachute payment, City will undoubtedly be one of the favourites to make a swift return but, as 2007/08 showed, the Championship is a difficult playing environment. City should make the top six and certainly should be pushing for one of the automatic promotion places.

Advance Tickets Tel No: 0871 557 1875
Fax: 0121 766 7866
Training Ground: Wasts Hall, Redhill Road, Kings Norton, Birmingham B38 9EJ. 0121 244 1401
Brief History: Founded 1875, as Small Heath Alliance. Changed to Small Heath in 1888, Birmingham in 1905, Birmingham City in 1945. Former Grounds: Arthur Street, Ladypool Road, Muntz Street, moved to St Andrew's in 1906. Record attendance 66,844.
(Total) Current Capacity: 30,016 (all seated)
Visiting Supporters' Allocation: 3-4,500 in new Railway End (Lower Tier)
Club Colours: Blue and white shirts, white shorts
Nearest Railway Station: Bordesley
Parking (Car): Street parking
Parking (Coach/Bus): Coventry Road
Police Force and Tel No: West Midlands (0121 772 1169)
Disabled Visitors' Facilities:
Wheelchairs: 90 places; advanced notice required
Blind: Commentary available
Future Development(s): The proposals for the Digbeth ground have not progressed and any future development is likely to involve work at St Andrews, where there are plans for the possible redevelopment of the Main Stand to take the ground's capacity to 36,500. There is no timescale for the £12 million project and with the club's relegation from the Premier League every possibility that it will be deferred.

season 07/08: FA Premier League **19th** (relegated) p38 w8 d11 l19 gf46 ga62

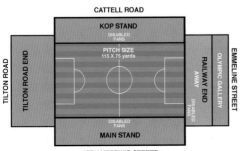

blackburn rovers

Ewood Park, Blackburn, Lancashire, BB2 4JF

website: **WWW.ROVERS.PREMIUMTV.CO.UK**
e:mail: **COMMERCIAL@ROVERS.CO.UK**
tel no: **0871 702 1875**
colours: **BLUE AND WHITE HALVED SHIRTS, WHITE SHORTS**
nickname: **ROVERS**
season 2008/09: **PREMIER LEAGUE**

One of the teams that spent the season challenging for the bragging rights of finishing top of the alternative Premier League for the right to finish fifth and thus grab a UEFA Cup spot, Rovers ultimately finished in seventh position. Under Mark Hughes, Rovers has become one of the more reliable of the teams competing in the top half of the Premier League; unlikely ever now to be able to break consistently into the monopoly that has developed within the top four, Rovers will always be capable of finishing close to the top of the rest but its best opportunity for silverware may well come through one of the cup competitions – as Portsmouth and Tottenham proved successfully in 2006/07. However, Mark Hughes' departure and the arrival of new manager Paul Ince along with the possible loss of influential players such as David Bentley means some uncertainty for the start of the new season.

Advance Tickets Tel No: 0871 222 1444

Fax: 01254 671042

Training Ground: Brockhall Training Ground, The Avenue, Brockhall Village, Blackburn BB6 8AW

Brief History: Founded 1875. Former Grounds: Oozebooth, Pleasington Cricket Ground, Alexandra Meadows. Moved to Ewood Park in 1890. Founder members of Football League (1888). Record attendance 61,783

(Total) Current Capacity: 31,367

Visiting Supporters' Allocation: 3,914 at the Darwen End

Nearest Railway Station: Blackburn

Parking (Car): Street parking and c800 spaces at ground

Parking (Coach/Bus): As directed by Police

Police Force and Tel No: Lancashire (01254 51212)

Disabled Visitors' Facilities:
Wheelchairs: All sides of the ground
Blind: Commentary available

Anticipated Development(s): There remain plans to redevelop the Riverside (Walker Steel) Stand to take Ewood Park's capacity to c40,000, but there is no confirmation as to if and when this work will be undertaken.

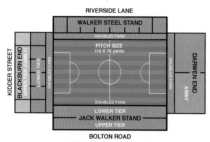

C Club Offices
S Club Shop
E Entrance(s) for visiting
supporters
R Refreshment bars for visiting
supporters
T Toilets for visiting supporters

1 A666 Bolton Road
2 Kidder Street
3 Nuttall Street
4 Town Centre & Blackburn
Central BR station
(1½ miles)
5 To Darwen and Bolton
6 Darwen End
7 Car Parks
8 Top O'Croft Road

⬆ *North direction (approx)*

◄ 698991
▼ 698999

1. Car Park
2. To Blackpool South BR Station (1½ miles) and M55 Junction 4
3. Bloomfield Road
4. Central Drive
5. Henry Street
6. East Stand (away)
7. Site of South Stand
8. West (Pricebusters Matthews) Stand
9. North Stand

⬆ *North direction (approx)*

▶ 701348
▼ 701352

blackpool

Bloomfield Road, Seasiders Way, Blackpool, FY1 6JJ

website: **WWW.BLACKPOOLFC.PREMIUMTV.CO.UK**
e:mail: **INFO@BLACKPOOLFC.CO.UK**
tel no: **0870 443 1953**
colours: **TANGERINE SHIRTS, WHITE SHORTS**
nickname: **THE SEASIDERS**
season 2008/09: **CHAMPIONSHIP**

Promoted via the Play-Offs at the end of the 2006/07 season, survival in the League Championship was always going to be the club's initial hope and, in terms of this ambition, the club was ultimately successful – although it was not until the final Sunday of the season that Championship status was assured. One of a number of teams that could have followed Colchester and Scunthorpe back to League One, Blackpool, along with Sheffield Wednesday, Southampton, Coventry and Leicester, could have been relegated if results had gone against the team. In the event, a 1-1 draw at Bloomfield Road with Play-off chasing Watford was sufficient to see Simon Grayson's team survive. Unless a severe bout of 'second seasonitis' kicks in, which did for Colchester United in 2007/08, Blackpool ought to have the potential to retain Championship status again but anything above a position of mid-table safety might be a bonus.

Advance Tickets Tel No: 0870 443 1953
Fax: 01253 405011
Training Ground: Squires Gate Training Ground, Martin Avenue, Lytham St Annes FY8 2SJ
Brief History: Founded 1887, merged with 'South Shore' (1899). Former grounds: Raikes Hall (twice) and Athletic Grounds, Stanley Park, South Shore played at Cow Cap Lane, moved to Bloomfield Road in 1899. Record attendance 38,098
Visiting Supporters' Allocation: 1,700 (all seated) in East Stand (open)
(Total) Current Capacity: 9,941 (All seated)
Club Colours: Tangerine shirts, white shorts
Nearest Railway Station: Blackpool South
Parking (Car): At Ground and street parking (also behind West Stand – from M55)
Parking (Coach/Bus): Mecca car park (behind North End (also behind West Stand – from M55)
Other Club Sharing Ground: Blackpool Panthers RLFC
Police Force and Tel No: Lancashire (01253 293933)
Disabled Visitors' Facilities:
Wheelchairs: North and West stands
Blind: Commentary available (limited numbers)
Anticipated Development(s): The go-ahead has been given to the construction of the new South Stand, although whether this is a temporary structure (similar to that already erected on the east of the ground) or a permanent structure has yet to be determined. It is likely that any new structure will initially lack a roof.

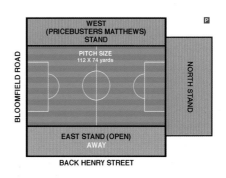

WEST
(PRICEBUSTERS MATTHEWS)
STAND

PITCH SIZE
112 X 74 yards

BLOOMFIELD ROAD

NORTH STAND

EAST STAND (OPEN)
AWAY

BACK HENRY STREET

bolton wanderers

Reebok Stadium, Burnden Way, Lostock, Bolton BL6 6JW

website: **WWW.BWFC.PREMIUMTV.CO.UK**
e:mail: **RECEPTION@BWFC.CO.UK**
tel no: **01204 673 673**
colours: **WHITE SHIRTS, WHITE SHORTS**
nickname: **THE TROTTERS**
season 2008/09: **PREMIER LEAGUE**

Following the departure of Sammy Lee, only appointed in the summer, the club appointed the experienced Gary Megson, who had only recently taken over at Leicester, as the new manager. The appointment, not wholly welcomed by many of the Reebok faithful, saw Wanderers achieve an impressive 2-2 draw away at Bayern Munich in one of Megson's first games in charge. The doubters were further silenced by victory at the Reebok Stadium 1-0 over Manchester United with the mercurial Nicolas Anelka scoring the all-important goal. However, despite the UEFA Cup run, which was probably a distraction in terms of the most important element of the season (retaining Premier League status), results in the latter half of the season saw the Trotters once more dragged back into the relegation battle and again brought into sharp relief the debate about Megson's ability to keep the team up. However, a 2-0 victory over Sunderland in the penultimate game of the campaign at the Reebok Stadium effectively guaranteed Wanderers' status – it would have taken a series of freak scores to have seen the team demoted – which was just as well as the club's final match was away at title-chasing Chelsea. With the home team needing victory to put the pressure on Manchester United, to expect anything from the game might have been optimistic. Although Chelsea were all over Bolton like a rash, the Blues could only score a single goal and a last-minute equaliser gave Wanderers a share of the points. With the gap between the Championship and the Premier League getting ever greater – two of the three promoted teams from the 2006/07 season were relegated after only one season – Bolton's status should again be secure but much will depend upon Megson's ability in the transfer market.

Advance Tickets Tel No: 0871 871 2932
Fax: 01204 673773
Training Ground: Euxton Training Ground, Euxton Lane, Chorley PR7 6FA
Brief History: Founded 1874 as Christ Church; name changed 1877. Former grounds: Several Fields, Pikes Lane (1880-95) and Burnden Park (1895-1997). Moved to Reebok Stadium for 1997/98 season. Record attendance (Burnden Park): 69,912. Record attendance of 28,353 at Reebok Stadium
(Total) Current Capacity: 28,723
Visiting Supporters' Allocation: 5,200 maximum (South Stand)
Club Colours: White shirts, white shorts
Nearest Railway Station: Horwich Parkway
Parking (Car): 2,800 places at ground with up 3,000 others in proximity
Parking (Coach/Bus): As directed
Police Force and Tel No: Greater Manchester (01204 522466)
Disabled Visitors' Facilities:
Wheelchairs: c100 places around the ground
Blind: Commentary available
Anticipated Developments(s): The station at Horwich Parkway has now opened. There are currently no further plans for the development of the Reebok Stadium.

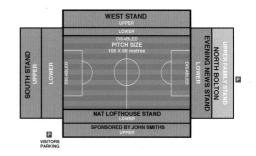

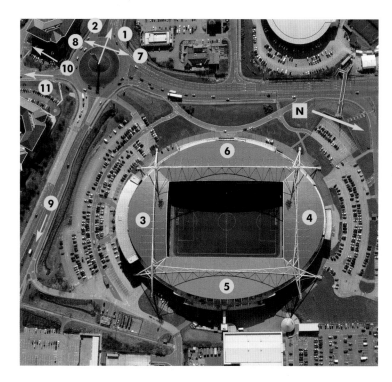

1 To Junction 6 of M61
2 A6027 Horwich link road
3 South Stand (away)
4 North Stand
5 Nat Lofthouse Stand
6 West Stand
7 M61 northbound to M6 and Preston (at J6)
8 M61 southbound to Manchester (at J6)
9 To Horwich and Bolton
10 To Lostock Junction BR station
11 To Horwich Parkway station

↑ North direction (approx)

◀ 700989
▼ 700996

C Club Offices

1 Car Park
2 A338 Wessex Way
3 To Bournemouth BR Station
  (1½ miles)
4 To A31 & M27
5 Thistlebarrow Road
6 King's Park Drive
7 Littledown Avenue
8 North Stand
9 Main Stand
10 East Stand
11 South Stand

↑ *North direction (approx)*

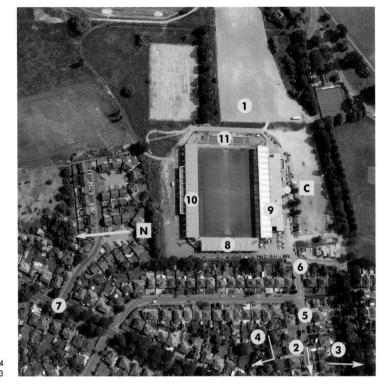

▶ 701244
▼ 701253

bournemouth

The Fitness First Stadium, Dean Court, Bournemouth, Dorset, BH7 7AF

website: **WWW.AFCB.PREMIUMTV.CO.UK**
e:mail: **ENQUIRIES@AFCB**
tel no: **01202 726300**
colours: **RED AND BLACK SHIRTS, BLACK SHORTS**
nickname: **THE CHERRIES**
season 2008/09: **LEAGUE TWO**

A season of considerable frustration and doubt at Dean Court saw the Cherries entering Administration and facing the distinct possibility that the club might fold. Having entered Administration, the team was automatically docked 10 points, which made an already hard campaign to avoid the drop into League Two all the more difficult. All credit, then, to Kevin Bond and the team, therefore, that the ultimate fate of the club was delayed for as long as it was; indeed it was not until the final day of the season that relegation was confirmed. Three teams – Bournemouth, Cheltenham and Crewe – all faced the possibility of dropping into League Two and, with Bournemouth's better goal difference, the team had the potential to survive. However, whilst Bournemouth were away at promotion-chasing Carlisle United, the other two teams were playing at home. Whilst Cheltenham secured their League One status with a hard-fought 2-1 win over Doncaster Rovers, Crewe seemed doomed with their 4-1 home defeat by Oldham if Bournemouth could grab a win at Carlisle. In the event, despite coming close, a 1-1 draw was not sufficient to keep the Cherries up. For 2008/09 there will be much uncertainty given that the club remained in Administration at the end of the current season and has been hit with a minus 15 point penalty for the start of the new season; provided that matters are speedily resolved then Kevin Bond can start to build for the new season but, as both Rotherham and Wrexham have shown, it can be a struggle to make an impact and relegation seems a likely result given the points deduction.

Advance Tickets Tel No: 01202 726303
Fax: 01202 726323
Training Ground: Canford School, Court House, Canford Magna, Wimborne BH21 3AF
Brief History: Founded 1890 as Boscombe St. John's, changed to Boscombe (1899), Bournemouth & Boscombe Athletic (1923) and A.F.C. Bournemouth (1971). Former grounds Kings Park (twice) and Castlemain Road, Pokesdown. Moved to Dean Court in 1910. Record attendance 28,799; since rebuilding: 10,375
(Total) Current Capacity: 10,700 (all seated)
Visiting Supporters' Allocation: 1,500 in East Stand (can be increased to 2,000 if required)
Nearest Railway Station: Bournemouth
Parking (Car): Large car park adjacent ground
Parking (Coach/Bus): Large car park adjacent ground
Police Force and Tel No: Dorset (01202 552099)
Disabled Visitors' Facilities:
Wheelchairs: 100 spaces
Blind: No special facility
Anticipated Development(s): The club still intends to construct a permanent South Stand at Dean Court, taking the ground's capacity to just under 12,000 but there is no confirmed schedule.

*relegated; 10 points deducted for going into Administration

season 07/08: League One **21ST*** (relegated) p**46** w**17** d**7** l**22** gf**62** ga**72**

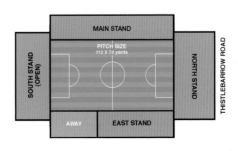

```
                    MAIN STAND
  ┌──────────────────────────────────────┐
  │                            PITCH SIZE │
  │ SOUTH STAND              112 X 74 yards │ NORTH STAND   THISTLEBARROW ROAD
  │ (OPEN)                                 │
  └──────────────────────────────────────┘
         AWAY        EAST STAND
```

bradford city

Coral Windows, Valley Parade, Bradford, BD8 7DY

website: **WWW.BRADFORDCITYFC.PREMIUMTV.CO.UK**
e:mail: **BRADFORDCITYFC@COMPUSERVE.COM**
tel no: **01274 773355**
colours: **CLARET AND AMBER SHIRTS, CLARET SHORTS**
nickname: **THE BANTAMS**
season 2008/09: **LEAGUE TWO**

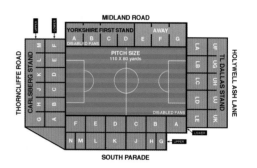

Relegated at the end of the 2006/07 season, the Bantams under new boss Stuart McCall were amongst the pre-season favourites for an immediate return to League One. However, a disappointing start to the campaign meant that the Valley Parade faithful were soon considering the fact that League Two wasn't the basement and that, without an improvement in form the Blue Square Premier was by no means an impossibility. The club's form picked up in the second half of the season and a late challenge for the Play-Offs was thwarted by the team's poor home form. City, through innovative marketing, had ensured that the home crowd was averaging some 13,000 during the season and this made the team's home form all the more difficult to understand. With the club now back on a more secure financial footing, expectations will be high that the new season will see a more dominant team at home and a more sustained push for automatic promotion.

Advance Tickets Tel No: 01274 770012

Fax: 01274 773356

Training Ground: Rawdon Meadows, Apperley Bridge, Bradford

Brief History: Founded 1903 (formerly Manningham Northern Union Rugby Club founded in 1876). Continued use of Valley Parade, joined 2nd Division on re-formation. Record attendance: 39,146

(Total) Current Capacity: 25,136

Visiting Supporters' Allocation: 1,130 (all seated) in Midland Stand

Club Colours: Claret and amber shirts, claret shorts

Nearest Railway Station: Bradford Forster Square

Parking (Car): Street parking and car parks

Parking (Coach/Bus): As directed by Police

Police Force and Tel No: West Yorkshire (01274 723422)

Disabled Visitors' Facilities:
Wheelchairs: 110 places in Sunwin, CIBA and Carlsberg stands; *Blind*: Commentary available

Anticipated Development(s): With work on the Main (Sunwin) Stand now completed, Valley Parade has a slightly imbalanced look. The club has proposals for the reconstruction of the Midland Road (Yorkshire First) Stand to take the ground's capacity to 30,000, although, given the club's current financial position, there is no time-scale.

C Club Offices
S Club Shop
E Entrance(s) for visiting
  supporters

1 Midland Road
2 Valley Parade
3 A650 Manningham Lane
4 To City Centre, Forster
  Square and Interchange BR
  Stations M606 & M62
5 To Keighley
6 Car Parks
7 Sunwin Stand
8 Midland (Yorkshire First)
  Stand
9 TL Dallas Stand
10 Carlsberg Stand

↑ North direction (approx)

◄ 700121
▼ 700114

C Club Offices
S Club Shop
E Entrance(s) for visiting
   supporters

1 Ealing Road
2 Braemar Road
3 Brook Road South
4 To M4 (¼ mile) & South
   Ealing Tube Station
   (1 mile)
5 Brentford BR Station
6 To A315 High Street & Kew
   Bridge
7 New Road
8 Ealing Road Terrace
9 Brook Road Stand (away)

⬆ *North direction (approx)*

▸ 701308
▾ 701306

brentford

Griffin Park, Breamar Road, Brentford, Middlesex, TW8 0NT

website: **WWW.BRENTFORDFC.PREMIUMTV.CO.UK**
e:mail: **ENQUIRIES@BRENTFORDFC.CO.UK**
tel no: **0845 3456 442**
colours: **RED AND WHITE STRIPES, BLACK SHORTS**
nickname: **THE BEES**
season 2008/09: **LEAGUE TWO**

Just before Christmas, with the Bees seemingly in free-fall down the League Two table after a reasonably promising start, Terry Butcher, who had only been appointed to the Griffin Park job during the summer, was sacked. He was replaced as caretaker by Andy Scott, under whom the team started to pick up some decent victories with the result that Scott was confirmed in the position as permanent manager in early January. Under the new manager the club's position was stabilised although a mid-table finish was ultimately to be considered a disappointment with the club finishing the lowest placed of the four teams relegated at the end of the 2006/07 season — even Rotherham with a 10-point deduction managed to finish above the Bees. For 2008/09 the club ought to have the potential to make a more sustained challenge for the Play-Offs but a top-half finish is perhaps the best that can be achieved.

Advance Tickets Tel No: 0845 3456 442
Fax: 020 8380 9937
Training Ground: Osterley Training Ground, 100 Jersey Road, Hounslow TW5 0TP
Brief History: Founded 1889. Former Grounds: Clifden House Ground, Benn's Field (Little Ealing), Shotters Field, Cross Roads, Boston Park Cricket Ground, moved to Griffin Park in 1904. Founder-members Third Division (1920). Record attendance 38,678
(Total) Current Capacity: 12,763 (8,905 seated)
Visiting Supporters' Allocation: 1,600 in Brook Road Stand (600 seated)
Club Colours: Red and white striped shirts, black shorts
Nearest Railway Station: Brentford, South Ealing (tube)
Parking (Car): Street parking (restricted)
Parking (Coach/Bus): Layton Road car park
Other Club Sharing Ground: Chelsea Reserves
Police Force and Tel No: Metropolitan (020 8577 1212)
Disabled Visitors' Facilities:
Wheelchairs: Braemar Road
Blind: Commentary available
Anticipated Development(s): Although the club still intends to relocate, a roof was installed over the Ealing Road Terrace in 2007 with home fans being transferred to that end. With a view to relocation, a site on Lionel Road has been identified although there is no confirmed timetable as to when or if work will commence.

brighton and hove albion

Withdean Stadium, Tongdean Lane, Brighton, BN1 5JD

website: **WWW.SEAGULLS.PREMIUMTV.CO.UK**
e:mail: **SEAGULLS@BHAFC.CO.UK**
tel no: **01273 695400**
colours: **BLUE AND WHITE STRIPED SHIRTS, WHITE SHORTS**
nickname: **THE SEAGULLS**
season 2008/09: **LEAGUE ONE**

A much-improved season for the Seagulls saw Dean Wilkins' team shake off the form of the previous season, where the club had been relegation candidates, to finish eventually in seventh place, just outside the Play-Offs. Never in with a serious shout of the Play-Offs, however, the club's late season form saw it gradually move up the League One table as the other potential Play-Off candidates at some stage — such as Tranmere and Leyton Orient — gradually slipped away. Following the end of the campaign, Dean Wilkins was replaced as manager by the experienced and well travelled Micky Adams, who was returning to a club he had managed before. Adams' experience should help the Seagulls make a more sustained push in 2008/09 but the Play-Offs are perhaps the best that the club can achieve.

Advance Ticket Tel No: 01273 776992
Fax: 01273 648179
Training Ground: University of Sussex, Falmer Sports Complex, Ridge Road, Falmer, Brighton BN1 9PL
Brief History: Founded 1900 as Brighton & Hove Rangers, changed to Brighton & Hove Albion 1902. Former grounds: Home Farm (Withdean), County Ground, Goldstone Ground (1902-1997), Priestfield Stadium (ground share with Gillingham) 1997-1999; moved to Withdean Stadium 1999. Founder members of the 3rd Division 1920. Record attendance (at Goldstone Ground): 36,747; at Withdean Stadium:8,691.

(Total) Current Capacity: 8,850 (all seated)
Visiting Supporters' Allocation: 900 max on open West Stand
Club Colours: Blue and white striped shirts, white shorts
Nearest Railway Station: Preston Park
Parking (Cars): Street parking in the immediate vicinity of the ground is residents' only. This will be strictly enforced and it is suggested that intending visitors should use parking facilities away from the ground and use the proposed park and ride bus services that will be provided.
Parking (Coach/Bus): As directed
Police Force and Tel No: Sussex (01273 778922)
Disabled Visitors' Facilities
Wheelchairs: Facilities in both North and South stands
Blind: No special facility

Anticipated Development(s): After a four-year campaign, permission for the construction of the new ground at Falmer was given by John Prescott at the end of October 2005. It was planned that work on the 23,000-seat capacity ground would start during 2006 with the intention of completion for the start of the 2007/08 season. However, Lewes District Council launched a legal challenge to the construction of the new ground and, in early March 2006, it was announced that this challenge would result in the ground being delayed with a new anticipated completion date of August 2009. A further development, on 6 April 2006, resulted in the original approval being quashed as a result of a mistake made in John Prescott's original letter of approval with the result that the matter would again have to be referred to him. In early July 2007 it was announced that £5.3 million had been awarded towards the cost of the construction of the ground from the South East England Development Agency provided that planning consent was given. Following the cabinet reshuffle, Hazel Blears gave the project the go-ahead at the end of July. Work is now scheduled to start on the new stadium during the 2008/9 season, with a completion date of mid-2010.

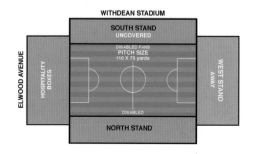

WITHDEAN STADIUM

| SOUTH STAND |
| UNCOVERED |

DISABLED FANS
PITCH SIZE
110 X 75 yards

ELWOOD AVENUE

HOSPITALITY BOXES

WEST STAND
AWAY

DISABLED

NORTH STAND

Shop Address:
6 Queen's Road, Brighton
Note: All games at Withdean will be
all-ticket with no cash
admissions on the day.

1 Withdean Stadium
2 London-Brighton railway line
3 To London Road (A23)
4 Tongdean Lane
5 Valley Drive
6 To Brighton town centre and
main railway station (1.75
miles)
7 Tongdean Lane (with bridge
under railway)
8 South Stand
9 A23 northwards to Crawley
10 To Preston Park railway station
11 North Stand
12 North East Stand
13 West Stand (away)

 North direction (approx)

◄ 699849
▼ 699861

C Club Offices
S Club Shop

1 A370 Ashton Road
2 A3209 Winterstoke Road
3 To Temple Meads Station
   (1½ miles)
4 To City Centre, A4,
   M32 & M4
5 Database Wedlock Stand
   (prior to redevelopment)
6 Atyeo Stand
7 Brunel Ford Williams Stand
8 Dolman Stand

⬆ *North direction (approx)*

▸ 699164
▾ 699177

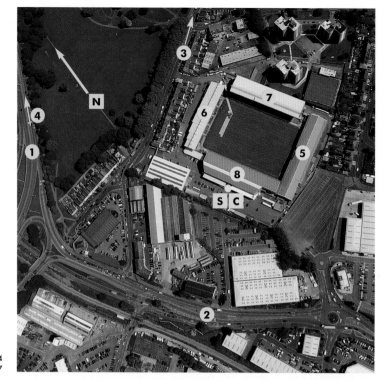

bristol city

Ashton Gate Stadium, Ashton Road, Bristol, BS3 2EJ

website: **WWW.BCFC.PREMIUMTV.CO.UK**
e:mail: **SALES@BCFC.CO.UK**
tel no: **0871 222 6666**
colours: **RED SHIRTS, WHITE SHORTS**
nickname: **THE ROBINS**
season 2008/09: **CHAMPIONSHIP**

Promoted at the end of the 2006/07 season, Gary Johnson's Bristol City team proved itself to be one of the surprise packages of the League Championship season, being one of the teams chasing an automatic promotion spot almost until the end of the season and then achieving a Play-Off place. Ultimately finishing in fourth place — only five points behind promoted Stoke City — the Robins faced Crystal Palace in the Play-Off semi-final. Under Neil Warnock, Palace had become one of the form teams in the second half of the season but a 2-1 victory at Selhurst Park gave Johnson's team the edge and, although Palace scored at Ashton Gate, two goals in extra time took City through to a final against another of the division's surprise packages — Hull City. Unfortunately for Bristol, Hull were to win 1-0 at Wembley, ensuring that Championship football will again be on offer at Ashton Gate in 2008/09. Potentially, City should again be a threat but — as other teams have discovered — the disappointment of a Play-Off defeat can lead to a struggle in the following season.

Advance Tickets Tel No: 0871 222 6666
Fax: 0117 963 0700
Training Ground: Abbots Leigh, Abbots Leigh Road, Bristol BS8 3QD
Brief History: Founded 1894 as Bristol South End changed to Bristol City in 1897. Former Ground: St John's Lane, Bedminster, moved to Ashton Gate in 1904. Record attendance 43,335
(Total) Current Capacity: 21,479 (all seated)
Visiting Supporters' Allocation: 3,000 in Micra Wedlock Stand (all seated; can be increased to 5,500 if necessary)
Nearest Railway Station: Bristol Temple Meads
Parking (Car): Street parking
Parking (Coach/Bus): Marsh Road
Police Force and Tel No: Avon/Somerset (0117 927 7777)
Disabled Visitors' Facilities:
Wheelchairs: Limited *Blind*: Commentary available
Anticipated Development(s): Although the club had previously been planning to redevelop its existing Ashton Gate ground, it was announced in late November 2007 that the club now favoured relocation. The new site, as yet at an undisclosed location close to Ashton Gate, is designed to accommodate a 30,000-seat stadium with the potential to have that increased to 40,000 in the event of the ground forming part of England's bid to host the 2018 World Cup. If all goes according to plan, the club will seek planning permission by the end of 2009 with the new ground available from the start of the 2011/12 season. Following relocation, Ashton Gate is likely to be sold for redevelopment.

season 07/08: Championship **4TH** p**46** w**20** d**14** l**12** gf**54** ga**53**

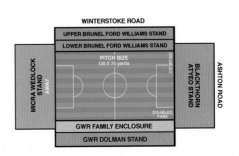

WINTERSTOKE ROAD

UPPER BRUNEL FORD WILLIAMS STAND

LOWER BRUNEL FORD WILLIAMS STAND

PITCH SIZE
120 X 75 yards

MICRA WEDLOCK STAND
AWAY

DISABLED

BLACKTHORN ATYEO STAND

ASHTON ROAD

DISABLED FANS

GWR FAMILY ENCLOSURE

GWR DOLMAN STAND

bristol rovers

The Memorial Stadium, Filton Avenue, Horfield, Bristol, BS7 0BF

website: **WWW.BRISTOLROVERS.PREMIUMTV.CO.UK**
e:mail: **FEEDBACK@BRISTOLROVERS.CO.UK**
tel no: **0117 909 6648**
colours: **BLUE AND WHITE QUARTERED SHIRTS, WHITE SHORTS**
nickname: **THE PIRATES (or Gasheads historically)**
season 2008/09: **LEAGUE ONE**

season 07/08: League One **16TH** p**46** w**12** d**17** l**17** gf**45** ga**53**

Promoted at the end of the 2006/07 season through the Play-Offs, the 2007/08 season was always going to be one of consolidation in League One for Rovers and, under Paul Trollope, this was achieved. Never seriously threatened with being drawn into the relegation battle, the club ultimately achieved a lower-half finish some five points above relegated Bournemouth. Away from the League, the club claimed the scalp of then struggling Championship side Crystal Palace at home on penalties in the 1st round of the Carling Cup and were also to defeat Premier League Fulham in the 3rd round of the FA Cup – again on penalties at the Memorial Stadium following an impressive drawn at Craven Cottage. For the new season, Rovers should again be able to make progress in League One and a top-half finish should not be an impossibility. The only potential dislocation might be caused by having to relocate temporarily during the course of the season if work on the redevelopment of the Memorial ground goes ahead.

Advance Tickets Tel No: 0117 909 8848
Fax: 0117 908 5530
Training Ground: Bristol Academy of Sport, Filton College, Filton Avenue, Bristol BS34 7AT
Brief History: Founded 1883 as Black Arabs, changed to Eastville Rovers (1884), Bristol Eastville Rovers (1896) and Bristol Rovers (1897). Former grounds: Purdown, Three Acres, The Downs (Horfield), Ridgeway, Bristol Stadium (Eastville), Twerton Park (1986-96), moved to The Memorial Ground 1996. Record attendance: (Eastville) 38,472, (Twerton Park) 9,813, (Memorial Ground) 11,433
(Total) Current Capacity: 11,917 (4,000 seated)
Visiting Supporters' Allocation: 1,132 (Centenary uplands Stand Terrace; open)
Nearest Railway Station: Filton or Stapleton Road
Parking (Car): Limited parking at ground for home fans only; street parking also available
Parking (Coach/Bus): As directed
Police Force and Tel No: Avon/Somerset (0117 927 7777)
Other Clubs Sharing Ground: Bristol Shoguns RUFC
Disabled Visitors' Facilities:
Wheelchairs: 35 wheelchair positions
Blind: Limited provision
Anticipated Development(s): As a result of changes to the original plans, the scheme for the redevelopment at the Memorial Ground has been delayed. Current plans envisaged work on the conversion of the ground into a new 18,500-seat facility, during which Bristol Rovers would ground share with Cheltenham Town — see pp52/53 — for about 18 months whilst work was completed. During summer 2008 the club announced a delay to the work with the result that the team will play at the Memorial Stadium for the 2008/09 season.
standing capacity of 8,000 includes 500 on the Family Terrace

MULLER ROAD
UPLANDS STAND
AWAY
DISABLED FANS
FILTON AVENUE
BASS TERRACE UNCOVERED
PITCH SIZE
110 X 74 yards
ELLICOTT ROAD
BASS SOUTH STAND
ALTON ROAD
DISABLED FANS
FAMILY TERRACE
WEST (DAS) STAND

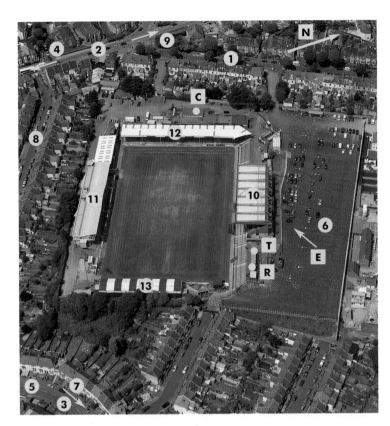

C Rugby Club offices
E Entrance(s) for visiting
  supporters
R Refrshments for visiting
  supporters
T Toilets for visiting supporters

1 Filton Avenue
2 Gloucester Road
3 To Muller Road
4 To Bristol city centre
  (2.5 miles) and BR Temple
  Meads station (3 miles)
5 Downer Road
6 Car Park
7 To M32 J2 (1½ miles)
8 Strathmore Road
9 To Filton (1½ miles)
10 Hill House Hammond Stand
11 West (Das) Stand
12 Blackthorn End
13 South Stand

↑ North direction (approx)

◄ 700378
▾ 700373

▲ 700160
▸ 700153

C Club Offices
S Club Shop
E Entrance(s) for visiting
supporters

1 Brunshaw Road
2 Belvedere Road
3 Burnley Central BR Station
(½ mile)
4 Cricket Ground
(David Fishwick)
5 Cricket Field Stand
6 East (Jimmy McIlroy) Stand
7 Bob Lord Stand
8 North (James Hargreaves)
Stand

⬆ *North direction (approx)*

burnley

Turf Moor, Harry Potts Way, Burnley, Lancashire, BB10 4BX

website: **WWW.BURNLEYFOOTBALLCLUB.PREMIUMTV.CO.UK**
e:mail: **INFO@BURNLEYFC.COM.**
tel no: **0871 221 1882**
colours: **CLARET AND BLUE SHIRTS, WHITE SHORTS**
nickname: **THE CLARETS**
season 2008/09: **CHAMPIONSHIP**

One of the teams that looked capable of mounting a sustained challenge for the Play-Offs at one stage, Steve Cotterill's Burnley side gradually drifted down the Championship table to finish ultimately in a disappointing 13th place. Unfortunately, with the nature of the modern Championship — with six teams always benefiting from the parachute payments from the Premier League and a number of other well-funded and highly ambitious teams endeavouring to reach the top-six paces, it's always going to be difficult over the length of a season for teams like Burnley to sustain a serious challenge and a top half position, with perhaps an outside shout of the Play-Offs, is the best that can be expected.

Advance Ticket No: 0871 221 1914
Fax: 01282 700014
Training Ground: Gawthorpe Hall, Off Padiham Road, Padiham, Burnley BB12 8UA
Brief History: Founded 1882, Burnley Rovers (Rugby Club) combined with another Rugby Club, changed to soccer and name to Burnley. Moved from Calder Vale to Turf Moor in 1882. Founder-members Football League (1888). Record attendance 54,775
(Total) Current Capacity: 22,546 (all seated)
Visiting Supporters' Allocation: 4,125 (all seated in David Fishwick [Cricket Field] Stand)
Nearest Railway Station: Burnley Central
Parking (Car): Church Street and Fulledge Rec. (car parks)
Parking (Coach/Bus): As directed by Police
Police Force and Tel No: Lancashire (01282 425001)
Disabled Visitors' Facilities:
Wheelchairs: Places available in North, East and Cricket Field stands
Blind: Headsets provided with commentary
Anticipated Development(s): Work is scheduled to start in the summer of 2008 — too late for recording photographically — on a £20 million scheme to rebuild the David Fishwick Stand into a new 2,500-seat single-tier stand and a new block between the Jimmy McIlroy and James Hargreaves stands for hospitality and changing rooms. This will be followed in 2009 by a refurbishment of the Bob Lord Stand. In order to allow for the work, away fans will be relocated to the lower tier of the Jimmy McIlroy Stand for the 2008/09 season.

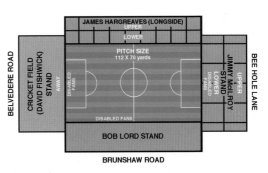

41

bury

Gigg Lane, Gigg Lane, Bury, Lancashire, BL9 9HR

website: **WWW.BURY.CO.UK**
e:mail: **INFO@BURYFC.CO.UK**
tel no: **0161 764 4881**
colours: **WHITE SHIRTS, ROYAL BLUE SHORTS**
nickname: **THE SHAKERS**
season 2008/09: **LEAGUE TWO**

In mid-January, following a 3-0 defeat by Darlington, Shakers' boss Chris Casper expressed concern for his position; his fears were well justified as early the following week Casper and the club's Director of Football, Keith Alexander, both departed from Gigg Lane. Chris Brass was appointed caretaker boss until early February when Alan Knill was appointed to the permanent position. Things started well for the new regime, with a 2-1 victory away at Bradford city in Knill's first match in charge representing the club's first league win since November. Under Knill the club's position improved and the team eventually finished in 13th position. Provided that this progress can be maintained in 2008/09 then the club should certainly have the potential to achieve a top-half finish.

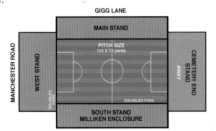

Advance Tickets Tel No: 0161 705 2144
Fax: 0161 764 5521
Training Ground: Lower Gigg, Gigg Lane, Bury BL9 9HR
Brief History: Founded 1885, no former names or former grounds. Record attendance 35,000
(Total) Current Capacity: 11,669 (all seated)
Visiting Supporters' Allocation: 2,500 (all seated) in Cemetery End Stand
Nearest Railway Station: Bury Interchange
Parking (Car): Street parking
Parking (Coach/Bus): As directed by Police
Police Force and Tel No: Greater Manchester (0161 872 5050)
Other clubs sharing ground:
FC United of Manchester
Disabled Visitors' Facilities:
Wheelchairs: South Stand (home) and West Stand (away)
Blind: Commentary available
Anticipated Development(s): The completion of the rebuilt Cemetery End means that current plans for the redevelopment of Gigg Lane have been completed.

C Club Offices
S Club Shop

1 Car Park
2 Gigg Lane
3 To A56 Manchester Road
4 To Town Centre & Bury
  Interchange (Metrolink)
  (¾ mile)
5 West (Manchester Road)
  Stand
6 Cemetery End (away)

↑ North direction (approx)

◀ 700091
▾ 700097

C Club Offices
S Club Shop
E Entrance(s) for visiting supporters
R Refreshment bars for visiting supporters
T Toilets for visiting supporters

1 Sloper Road
2 B4267 Leckwith Road
3 Car Park
4 To A4232 & M4 Junction 33 (8 miles)
5 Ninian Park Road
6 To City Centre & Cardiff Central BR Station (1 mile)
7 To A48 Western Avenue, A49M, and M4 Junction 32 and 29
8 Ninian Park BR station

↑ *North direction (approx)*

▸ 699068
▾ 699079

cardiff city

Ninian Park, Sloper Road, Cardiff, CF11 8SX

website: **WWW.CARDIFFCITYFC.PREMIUMTV.CO.UK**
e:mail: **CLUB@CARDIFFCITYFC.CO.UK**
tel no: **029 2022 1001**
colours: **BLUE SHIRTS, BLUE SHORTS**
nickname: **THE BLUEBIRDS**
season 2008/09: **CHAMPIONSHIP**

A season of considerable success for the Bluebirds both on and off the pitch saw work finally commence on the construction of the team's new stadium, some progress on the issue of the club's indebtedness and, in a season when the romance returned to the FA Cup, a trip to Wembley with the opportunity of taking the cup back to Cardiff as winners for the first time since the 1920s. In a season of shocks, Cardiff battled through to Wembley with a 2-0 victory away at Middlesbrough before defeating Barnsley — conquerors earlier of both Liverpool and Chelsea — in the semi-final. Unfortunately for Dave Jones' team, in final of relatively few clear cut chances, the opportunities that City had were squandered and the game was won by a single goal from Portsmouth's Kanu just before half time. In the League, City also started brightly although as the campaign wore on so the team drifted further away from the Play-Off spots ultimately finishing in 12th position. For the new season, much will depend Jones' success in retaining key players and how far the club will need to exploit emerging talent financially. With the new season representing probably the last year that football will be played at Ninian Park, fans will be hoping that the move to the new ground can be completed on a high but it's more likely that a top-half is the best that can be hoped for, with little likelihood of a return to Wembley in the FA Cup.

Advance Tickets Tel No: 0845 345 1400
Fax: 029 2034 1148
Training Ground: University of Glamorgan, Tyn-Y-Wern Playing Fields, Treforest Industrial Estate, Upper Boat, Pontypridd, CF37 5UP
Brief History: Founded 1899. Former Grounds: Riverside Cricket Club, Roath, Sophia Gardens, Cardiff Arms Park and The Harlequins Rugby Ground, moved to Ninian Park in 1910. Ground record attendance 61,566 (Wales v. England, 1961)
(Total) Current Capacity: 20,000 (12,647 seated)
Visiting Supporters' Allocation: 2,000 maximum in John Smiths Grange End Terrace (limited seating)
Club Colours: Blue shirts, blue shorts
Nearest Railway Station: Ninian Park (adjacent) (Cardiff Central 1 mile)
Parking (Car): Opposite Ground, no street parking around ground
Parking (Coach/Bus): Leckwith Stadium car park
Police Force and Tel No: South Wales (029 2022 2111)
Disabled Visitors' Facilities: *Wheelchairs:* Corner Canton Stand/Popular Bank (covered) *Blind:* No special facility
Anticipated Development(s): Work started on the development of the new £42 million stadium with the demolition of the Leckwith Stadium commencing at the end of October 2007. It is anticipated that the new ground, initially with a 25,000 seat capacity, will be available for the start of the 2009/10 season. The new ground will be shared with the Cardiff Blues RUFC club, who will move in from their existing ground at Cardiff Arms Park.

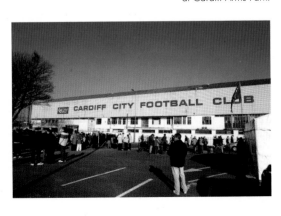

carlisle united

Brunton Park, Warwick Road, Carlisle, CA1 1LL

website: **WWW.CARLISLEUNITED.PREMIUMTV.CO.UK**
e:mail: **ENQUIRIES@CARLISLEUNITED.CO.UK**
tel no: **01228 526237**
colours: **BLUE SHIRTS, WHITE SHORTS**
nickname: **THE CUMBRIANS OR THE BLUES**
season 2008/09: **LEAGUE ONE**

The first management casualty of the new season occurred less than 48 hours after Carlisle United had played its first match of the season — a 1-1 draw away at promoted Walsall — when Neil McDonald was sacked as boss at Carlisle. He was replaced immediately by Greg Abbott as caretaker boss. Although Greg Abbott was widely tipped to take over as boss, the club raided League One rivals Cheltenham Town and made John Ward the new manager. Under Ward, United remained serious contenders for automatic promotion throughout the season and the club's ultimate fate was only determined on the final day of the season when three clubs — United, Nottingham Forest and Doncaster Rovers — were all capable of taking second spot behind Swansea City. Carlisle's draw at home to relegation threatened Bournemouth allied to Rovers' defeat and Forest's victory took the Midlands team up and consigned Carlisle and Doncaster to the Play-Offs. In the Play-Offs Carlisle faced Leeds United and a 2-1 victory at Elland Road seemed to have given Carlisle the edge, although a late Leeds goal gave the home team renewed hope which they built upon in the away leg at Brunton Park with a 2-0 victory. Defeated 3-2 on aggregate, Carlisle face another season in League One but should again have the potential to mount a challenge for the Play-Offs.

Advance Tickets Tel No: 01228 526327
Fax: 01228 554141
Training Ground: Adjacent to main ground
Brief History: Founded 1904 as Carlisle United (previously named Shaddongate United). Former Grounds: Millholme Bank and Devonshire Park, moved to Brunton Park in 1909. Record attendance 27,500
(Total) Current Capacity: 16,98 (6,433 seated)
Visiting Supporters' Allocation: 1,700 (Petterill End Terrace — open — or north end of Main Stand)
Nearest Railway Station: Carlisle
Parking (Car): Rear of ground
Parking (Coach/Bus): St Aiden's Road car park
Police Force and Tel No: Cumbria (01228 528191)
Disabled Visitors' Facilities:
Wheelchairs: East Stand and Paddock (prior arrangement)
Blind: No special facilities

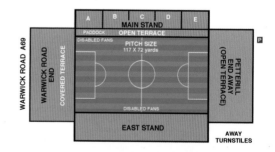

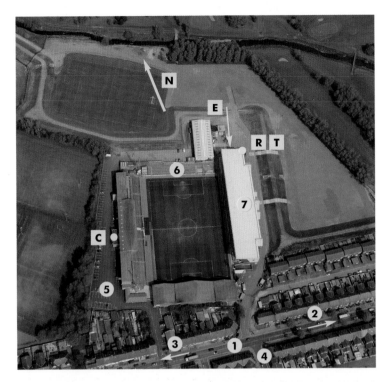

C Club Offices
E Entrance(s) for visiting supporters
R Refreshment bars for visiting supporters
T Toilets for visiting supporters

1 A69 Warwick Road
2 To M6 Junction 43
3 Carlisle Citadel BR station (1 mile)
4 Greystone Road
5 Car Park
6 Petterill End (away)
7 Cumberland Bulding Society (East) Stand

⬆ North direction (approx)

◀ 701256
▼ 701264

E Entrance(s) for visiting
supporters

R Refreshment bars for visiting
supporters

T Toilets for visiting supporters

1 Harvey Gardens
2 A206 Woolwich Road
3 Valley Grove
4 Floyd Road
5 Charlton BR Station
6 East Stand
7 North Stand
8 West stand
9 South stand (away)
10 Charlton Church Lane
11 Charlton Lane

⬆ *North direction (approx)*

▸701309
▾701316

charlton athletic
The Valley, Floyd Road, Charlton, London, SE7 8BL

website: **WWW.CAFC.CO.UK**
e:mail: **CUSTOMERSERVICES@CAFC.CO.UK**
tel no: **020 8333 4000**
colours: **RED SHIRTS, WHITE SHORTS**
nickname: **THE ADDICKS**
season 2008/09: **CHAMPIONSHIP**

Relegated at the end of the 2006/07 season, Alan Pardew's Charlton Athletic were widely considered to be amongst the favourites to reach the Play-Offs at least. In the event, however, the club had a disappointing season, ultimately finishing in 11th place, albeit only six points off Watford in sixth place. In a tight division nine points covered Crystal Palace in fifth through to Burnley in 13th and each of the teams in these positions had opportunities to sustain a challenge but for the most part failed to do so. The new season will be the second and last of those in which Charlton will receive a parachute payment from the Premier League and is thus perhaps the final opportunity to mount a serious push for promotion or the Play-Offs. However, with two strong teams and Derby County being relegated, Athletic's route back to the top flight may well be through the Play-Offs.

Advance Tickets Tel No: 0871 226 1905
Fax: 020 8333 4001
Training Ground: Sparrows Lane, New Eltham, London SE9 2JR
Brief History: Founded 1905. Former grounds: Siemens Meadows, Woolwich Common, Pound Park, Angerstein Athletic Ground, The Mount Catford, Selhurst Park (Crystal Palace FC), Boleyn Ground (West Ham United FC), The Valley (1912-23, 1924-85, 1992-date). Founder Members 3rd Division South. Record attendance 75,031
(Total) Current Capacity: 27,116(all seated)
Visiting Supporters' Allocation: 3,000 (maximum; all seated in South Stand)
Nearest Railway Station: Charlton
Parking (Car): Street parking
Parking (Coach/Bus): As directed by Police
Police Force and Tel No: Metropolitan (020 8853 8212)
Disabled Visitors' Facilities:
Wheelchairs: East/West/South stands
Blind: Commentary, 12 spaces
Anticipated Development(s): The club presented plans to Greenwich Council in mid-December 2006 for the redevelopment of the East Stand, taking the ground's capacity to 31,000. At the same time the club lodged outline plans for the redevelopment of the rest of the stadium with the intention of taking capacity to 40,600.

season 07/08: Championship **11TH** p46 w17 d13 l16 gf63 ga58

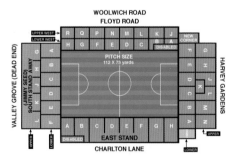

chelsea

Stamford Bridge, Fulham Road, London, SW6 1HS

website: **WWW.CHELSEAFC.COM**
e:mail: **CONTACT VIA WEBSITE**
tel no: **0871 984 1951**
colours: **BLUE SHIRTS, BLUE SHORTS**
nickname: **THE BLUES**
season 2008/09: **PREMIER LEAGUE**

At the start of the season, the hot favourite to be the first managerial casualty in the Premier League was Wigan boss, Chris Hutchings. In the event, however, the increasingly fractious relationship between Jose Mourinho and other influential figures at Stamford Bridge resulted in the departure of 'The Special One' following a series of three disappointing results: defeat away at Aston Villa followed by home draws against Blackburn and Rosenborg in mid-September. The club moved quickly to appoint Avram Grant, recruited in the close season as Director of Football, as the new boss. It was, however, a strange appointment with rumours about his replacement starting almost from the off. On the field, Grant proved to be reasonably successful in all competitions, taking the team to the Carling Cup final (where Chelsea were defeated by Tottenham) and to the FA Cup quarter-finals (where they were defeated by Championship side Barnsley). But it was in the League and Champions League where Grant had most success. In the former, the competition went right to the wire with results on the final day resulting in the title ultimately going to Manchester United, and in the latter, but for John Terry's slip in the penalty shootout, the cup would have been heading for Stamford Bridge rather than Old Trafford. Thus, despite an impressive record that saw his team win 36 out of 54 competitive matches and only lose five, Grant was unceremoniously dismissed shortly after the Champions League final. New manager Luis Felipe Scolari knows how ambitious Roman Abramovich is for the club; ultimately it comes down to two alternatives: success or the sack. The Blues will undoubtedly be again one of the major forces at home and abroad but silverware may yet again prove elusive.

Advance Tickets Tel No: 0871 984 1905
Fax: 020 7381 4831
Training Ground: 62 Stoke Road, Cobham, Surrey KT11 3PT
Brief History: Founded 1905. Admitted to Football League (2nd Division) on formation. Stamford Bridge venue for F.A. Cup Finals 1919-22. Record attendance 82,905
(Total) Current Capacity: 42,449 (all seated)
Visiting Supporters' Allocation: Approx. 1,600 (East Stand Lower; can be increased to 3,200 if required or 5,200 if part of the Matthew Harding Stand [lower tier] is allocated)
Nearest Railway Station: Fulham Broadway or West Brompton
Parking (Car): Street parking and underground car park at ground
Parking (Coach/Bus): As directed by Police
Police Force and Tel No: Metropolitan (020 7385 1212)
Disabled Visitors' Facilities:
Wheelchairs: East Stand;
Blind: No special facility

Anticipated Development(s): Faced by the competing clubs building ever larger grounds, Chelsea is conscious that the existing 42,000-seat capacity at Stamford Bridge is too small but difficult to increase. As a result the club is examining the possibility of relocation, with a number of sites (including the erstwhile Lillie Bridge cricket ground now used as the Seagrave Road car park as one option). There is, however, no definite plan as yet nor any timetable for the work if it were to proceed.

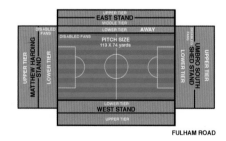

FULHAM ROAD

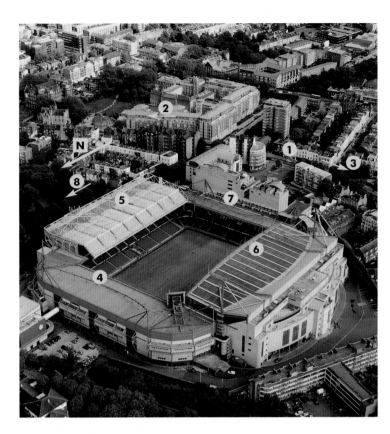

1 A308 Fulham Road
2 Central London
3 To Fulham Broadway Tube
   Station
4 Matthew Harding Stand
5 East Stand
6 West Stand
7 South (Shed) Stand
8 West Brompton Station

↑ *North direction (approx)*

◄ 700208
▼ 700211

C Club Offices
E Entrance(s) for visiting
supporters

1 B4632 Prestbury Road
2 Cromwell Road
3 Whaddon Road
4 Wymans Road
5 To B4075 Priors Road
6 To B4075 Prior Road
7 To Cheltenham town centre
and railway station (1.5 and
2 miles respectively)
8 Main Stand
9 Wymans Road Stand
10 Prestbury Road End
11 Carlsberg Stand (away)

↑ *North direction (approx)*

▶ 699755
▼ 699762

cheltenham town

Whaddon Road, Cheltenham, Gloucestershire GL52 5NA

website: **CHELTENHAMTOWNFC.PREMIUMTV.CO.UK**
e:mail: **INFO@CTFC.COM**
tel no: **01242 573558**
colours: **RED AND WHITE STRIPED SHIRTS, WHITE SHORTS**
nickname: **THE ROBINS**
season 2008/09: **LEAGUE ONE**

Following John Ward's departure to take over as boss at high-flying Carlisle United at the end of September, Keith Downing was appointed as caretaker boss at Whaddon Road. In early November, it was confirmed that Downing had been handed the job on a permanent basis. The club spent much of the season in or around the League One drop zone and the club's status was still in doubt right through until the final Saturday of the season. With four teams facing the drop to League Two — Crewe, Bournemouth and Gillingham were also threatened — Town, who started the match in the all-important 20th place knew that a home win over promotion chasing Doncaster Rovers would ensure League One status irrespective of results elsewhere. Although Doncaster undoubtedly could have upset the party, a 2-1 win ensured that League One football will again be on the agenda at Whaddon Road in 2008/09 but, with ambitious teams such as MK Dons and Peterborough emerging from League Two, it could be another struggle to avoid the drop in the new season and a struggle that could prove too great for the team.

Advance Tickets Tel No: 01242 573558
Fax: 01242 224675
Training Ground: Cheltenham Town FC Training Complex, Quat Goose Lane, Swindon Village, Cheltenham GL51 9RX
Brief History: Cheltenham Town was founded in 1892. It moved to Whaddon Road in 1932 having previously played at Carter's Field. After two seasons in the Conference it achieved Nationwide League status at the end of the 1998/99 season. Record attendance 8,326
(Total) Current Capacity: 7,006 (3,912 seated)
Visiting Supporters' Allocation: 2,600 (maximum) in Carlsberg (Whaddon Road) Stand – and in Wymans Road (In2Print) Stand
Nearest Railway Station: Cheltenham (1.5 miles)
Parking (Car): Limited parking at ground; otherwise on-street
Parking (Coach/Bus): As directed by Police
Police Force and Tel No: Gloucestershire (01242 521321)
Disabled Visitors' Facilities: *Wheelchairs*: Six spaces in front of Main Stand *Blind*: No special facility
Anticipated Development(s): The Carlsberg stand — which replaced the open Whaddon Road Terrace — was opened in December 2005. This structure provides seats for 1,000 fans. The next phase in the development of Whaddon Road will involve the rebuilding of the Main Stand, but there is at present no timescale for this work.

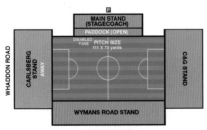

chester city

Deva Stadium, Bumpers Lane, Chester, CH1 4LT

website: **WWW.CHESTERCITYFC.NET**
e:mail: **CONTACT VIA WEBSITE**
tel no: **01244 371376**
colours: **BLUE AND WHITE SHIRTS, WHITE SHORTS**
nickname: **THE BLUES**
season 2008/09: **LEAGUE TWO**

After less than a year in charge at City, manager Billy Williamson departed the Deva Stadium in early March following a run of only one win in 14 league games culminating in a 1-0 away defeat at high-flying Milton Keynes Dons after a promising start to the campaign had seen the team vying for a Play-Off place. Simon Davey, the youth team coach, took over as caretaker boss. Under Davey the club's drift down the League Two table continued and it was by no means certain that the club was going to maintain its League status as both Mansfield and Wrexham started to pick up points. However, 0-0 draws in the last two games of the season — away at local rivals Shrewsbury Town (where both sets of fans were able to celebrate the demise of Wrexham) and at home to Macclesfield — meant that City were secure irrespective of Mansfield's last result. Unless there is a dramatic reversal of form come the new season, it looks as though Chester will again struggle in League Two and a further battle to avoid the drop cannot be ruled out.

Advance Tickets Tel No: 01244 371376
Fax: 01244 390265
Training Ground: Chester Catholic High School, Old Wrexham Road, Chester CH4 7HS
Brief History: Founded 1884 from amalgamation of Chester Wanderers and Chester Rovers. Former Grounds: Faulkner Street, Lightfoot Street, Whipcord Lane, Sealand Road Moss Lane (Macclesfield Town FC), moved to Deva Stadium 1992. Record attendance (Sealand Road) 20,500; (Deva Stadium) 5,987
(Total) Current Capacity: 5,376 (4,170 seated)
Visiting Supporters' Allocation: 1,200 (all-seated) in South and West stands
Nearest Railway Station: Chester (three miles)
Parking (Car): Car park at ground
Parking(Coach/Bus): Car park at ground
Police Force and Tel No: Cheshire (01244 350222)
Disabled Visitors' Facilities:
Wheelchairs: West and East Stand
Blind: Facility available

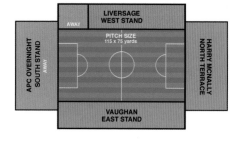

C Club Offices
S Club Shop
E Entrance(s) for visiting supporters
R Refreshment bars for visiting supporters
T Toilets for visiting supporters

1 Bumpers Lane
2 To City centre and Chester railway station (1.5 miles)
3 Car park
4 South Terrace
5 West Stand

↑ North direction (approx)

◄ 700510
▼ 700517

C Club Offices
S Club Shop
E Entrance(s) for visiting supporters
R Refreshment bars for visiting supporters
T Toilets for visiting supporters

1 Saltergate
2 Cross Street
3 St Margaret's Drive
4 West Bars
5 To A617 & M1 Junction 29
6 To station and town centre
7 Compton Street Terrace
8 Cross Street End

↑ North direction (approx)

▸ 701043
▾ 701047

chesterfield

Recreation Ground, Saltergate, Chesterfield, S40 4SX

website: **WWW.CHESTERFIELD–FC.PREMIUMTV.CO.UK**
e:mail: **SUEGREEN@CHESTERFIELD–FC.CO.UK**
tel no: **01246 209765**
colours: **BLUE AND WHITE SHIRTS, WHITE SHORTS**
nickname: **THE SPIREITES**
season 2008/09: **LEAGUE TWO**

Under Lee Richardson, the Spireites made a decent attempt to reclaim the League One position lost at the end of the 2006/07 campaign. Never good enough to mount a sustained challenge for automatic promotion, the club was in the hunt for the Play-Offs until towards the end of the season. However, although finishing in eighth place, the team ended up nine points adrift of Wycombe in the all-important seventh place. Provided that Richardson can build upon his squad there is every possibility that Chesterfield will again be one of those vying for a Play-Off place in 2008/09.

Advance Tickets Tel No: 01246 209765
Fax: 01246 556799
Training Ground: No special facility
Brief History: Found 1886. Former Ground: Spital Vale. Formerly named Chesterfield Town. Record attendance 30,968
(Total) Current Capacity: 8,504 (2,674 seated)
Visiting Supporters' Allocation: 1,850 maximum (maximum 450 seated)
Nearest Railway Station: Chesterfield
Parking (Car): Saltergate car park, street parking
Parking (Coach/Bus): As directed by Police
Police Force and Tel No: Derbyshire (01246 220100)
Disabled Visitors' Facilities:
Wheelchairs: Saltergate Stand
Blind: No special facility
Anticipated Development(s): The club is progressing with plans for the construction of a new 10,600-seat ground on the site of the closed Dema glassworks on the A61. However, physical work on the site has been delayed as a result of land ownership for part of the site. Despite this, the club remains hopeful that the new ground will be completed in time for the start of the 2009/10 season, with a successful planning application submitted in early July 2008.

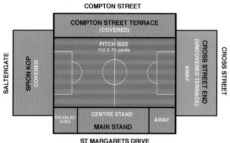

colchester united

Weston Homes Community Stadium

website: **WWW.CU–FC.PREMIUMTV.CO.UK**
e:mail: **CAROLINE@COLCHESTERUNITED.NET**
tel no: **0871 226 2161***
colours: **BLUE AND WHITE SHIRTS, WHITE SHORTS**
nickname: **THE U'S**
season 2008/09: **LEAGUE ONE**

Following the sale of the club's two main strikers at the end of the 2006/07 season, the new season was always likely to be a struggle for Geraint Williams' squad. In the event that proved to be the case, although — surprisingly — it wasn't a lack of fire power up front that did for the team but a tendency to ship vast numbers of goals at the back. Thus, in a severe case of second-seasonitis, the Us were relegated back to League One and thus will launch the club's career in its new ground in football's third tier. However, with the optimism that occupation of the new ground will bring, United should have the potential to make a serious play for promotion back to the League Championship. However, there are a number of equally ambitious clubs at this level and perhaps a Play-Off place is perhaps the best that can be hoped for.

Advance Tickets Tel No: 081 226 2161*

Fax: 01206 715327*

* These are the numbers for Layer Road and may change with the move.

Training Ground: No special facility

Brief History: Founded 1937, joined Football League 1950, relegated 1990 to Conference, promoted back to the Football League 1992. Played at Layer Road until end of 2007/08 season. Record attendance (at Layer Road) 19,072

(Total) Current Capacity: 10,000 (all seated)

Visiting Supporters' Allocation: tbc

Nearest Railway Station: Colchester main line (two miles)

Parking (Car): 600 spaces at ground

Parking (Coach/Bus): As directed

Police Force and Tel No: Essex (01206 762212)

Disabled Visitors' Facilities:

Wheelchairs: 100 wheelchair places; *Blind*: tbc

Anticipated Development(s): Following a number of years planning for relocation, the club played its final season at its old Layer Road ground in 2007/08 and relocated to the new £14 million 10,000-seat stadium for the start of the 2008/09 campaign. The ground is designed to allow for expansion to 18,000 if the need arises.

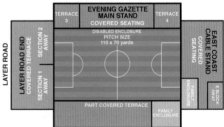

1 A12
2 Towards intersection with new northern link road and Ipswich
3 Towards London
4 To Colchester town centre (three miles) and Colchester main line station
5 North Stand
6 East Stand
7 West Stand
8 South Stand

↑ North direction (approx)

◄ 701205
▼ 701208

coventry city

The Ricoh Arena, Phoenix Way, Foleshill, Coventry CV6 6GE

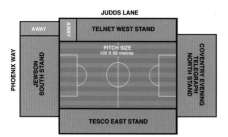

JUDDS LANE

AWAY | AWAY | TELNET WEST STAND

PHOENIX WAY

JEWSON SOUTH STAND

PITCH SIZE
105 X 68 metres

COVENTRY EVENING TELEGRAPH NORTH STAND

TESCO EAST STAND

website: **WWW.CCFC.PREMIUMTV.CO.UK**
e:mail: **MARK.DAVIES@CCFC.CO.UK**
tel no: **0870 421 1987**
colours: **SKY BLUE SHIRTS, SKY BLUE SHORTS**
nickname: **THE SKY BLUES**
season 2008/09: **CHAMPIONSHIP**

Advance Tickets Tel No: 0870 421 1987
Fax: 0870 421 5073
Training Ground: Sky Blue Lodge, Leamington Road, Ryton-on-Dunsmore, Coventry CV8 3EL
Brief History: Founded 1883 as Singers FC, changed name to Coventry City in 1898. Former grounds: Dowell's Field, Stoke Road Ground and Highfield Road (1899-2005) moved to new ground for start of the 2005/06 season. Record attendance (at Highfield Road): 51,455; (at Ricoh Stadium) 28,163
(Total) Current Capacity: 32,500 (all seated)
Visiting Supporters' Allocation: 3,000 in corner of Jewson South and Telnet West Stands
Nearest Railway Station: Coventry (three miles)
Parking (Car): As directed
Parking (Coach/Bus): As directed
Police Force and Tel No: West Midlands (02476 539010)
Disabled Visitors' Facilities:
Wheelchairs: 102 spaces (including 27 away) at pitchside or raised platform
Blind: no special facility at present but under negotiation
Anticipated Development(s): With the completion of the Ricoh Stadium there are no further plans for development at the present time. There is still no news about the construction of a possible station on the Coventry-Nuneaton railway line.

In mid-February, just after a 1-0 defeat away at fellow strugglers that left City only four points above the Championship drop-zone, Iain Dowie was sacked as manager. He was replaced, on a caretaker basis, by Frankie Bunn and John Harbin. In mid-February the club announced the appointment of ex-Fulham boss Chris Coleman as the new manager following his brief sojourn as manager of Real Sociedad in Spain. Under Coleman City retained its League Championship position — but only just. Had results gone differently on the final day it could have been Coventry rather than Leicester heading for League One. Coventry's 4-1 trouncing away at Charlton was dire but Leicester's 0-0 draw away at Stoke City meant that the Sky Blues survived by only a single point (and with an infinitely worse goal difference). Away from the League, there was one high point in Dowie's reign as City boss: the 4-1 victory at Ewood Park over Blackburn Rovers in the 3rd round of the FA Cup. As with other ex-Premier League teams that have lost the parachute payments, Coventry now struggle to make an impact at this level and, depending on Coleman's ability to attract players to the team, a position of mid-table mediocrity is perhaps the best that the team can look forward to.

RICOH

crewe alexandra

The Alexandra Stadium, Gresty Road, Crewe, Cheshire, CW2 6EB

website: **WWW.CREWEALEX.PREMIUMTV.CO.UK**
e:mail: **INFO@CREWEALEX.NET**
tel no: **01270 213014**
colours: **RED SHIRTS, WHITE SHORTS**
nickname: **THE RAILWAYMEN**
season 2008/09: **LEAGUE ONE**

season 07/08: League One **21ST** p**46** w**12** d**14** l**20** gf**47** ga**65**

With much respected Dario Gradi now promoted to be the club's Technical Director, new first-team coach Steve Holland had the task of trying to restore Alexandra's fortunes. Unfortunately, however, the club seemed more interested in escaping through the League One trapdoor rather than making a serious attempt at even mid-table and on the last day of the season Crewe's League One status was not assured. One of four teams vying to avoid filling the final two relegation spots — the others being Bournemouth, Cheltenham and Gillingham — the Railwaymen knew that their home game against Oldham was critical. However, a 4-1 defeat at Gresty Road meant that the team was sweating on results elsewhere. Cheltenham's victory allied to Bournemouth's draw at Carlisle and Gillingham's defeat at Leeds United, meant that Crewe survived in League One for a further season (although the club needs to be thankful that Bournemouth had been docked 10 points for going into Administration; without this penalty Bournemouth would have survived and Crewe would now be facing games against Aldershot). However, with ambitious and well-funded teams coming up from League Two, Crewe's ability to survive at this level may well be again threatened in 2008/09.

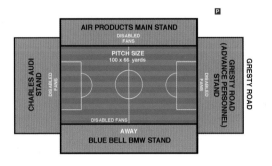

Advance Tickets Tel No: 01270 252610
Fax: 01270 216320
Training Ground: Details omitted at club's request
Brief History: Founded 1877. Former Grounds: Alexandra Recreation Ground (Nantwich Road), Earle Street Cricket Ground, Edleston Road, Old Sheds Fields, Gresty Road (Adjacent to current Ground), moved to current Ground in 1906. Founder members of 2nd Division (1892) until 1896. Founder members of 3rd Division North (1921). Record attendance 20,000
(Total) Current Capacity: 21,479 (all seated)
Visiting Supporters' Allocation: 1,694 (Blue Bell BMW Stand)
Nearest Railway Station: Crewe
Parking (car): There is a car park adjacent to the ground. It should be noted that there is a residents' only scheme in operation in the streets surrounding the ground.
Parking (Coach/Bus): As directed by Police
Police Force and Tel No: Cheshire (01270 500222)
Disabled Visitors' Facilities:
Wheelchairs: Available on all four sides
Blind: Commentary available
Anticipated Development(s): The club has long term plans for the construction of a new two-tier stand to replace the Blue Bell (BMW) Stand, although there is no confirmed timescale for the work.

C Club Offices
S Club Shop
E Entrance(s) for visiting
   supporters

1 Crewe BR Station
2 Gresty Road
3 Gresty Road
4 A534 Nantwich Road
5 To A5020 to
   M6 Junction 16
6 To M6 Junction 17 [follow
   directions at roundabout to
   M6 J16/J17]
7 Main (Air Products) Stand
8 Gresty Road (Advance
   Personnel) Stand
9 Charles Audi Stand
10 Ringways Stand
   (Blue Bell BMW)(away)
11 Car Park

⬆ North direction (approx)

◄ 700949
▼ 700955

C Club Offices
S Club Shop
E Entrance(s) for visiting supporters
T Toilets for visiting supporters

1 Whitehorse Lane
2 Park Road
3 Arthur Wait Stand Road
4 Selhurst BR Station (½ mile)
5 Norwood Junction BR Station (¼ mile)
6 Thornton Heath BR Station (½ mile)
7 Car Park (Sainsbury's)

↑ North direction (approx)

▸ 700223
▾ 700220

crystal palace

Selhurst Park, London, SE25 6PU

website: **WWW.CPFC.PREMIUMTV.CO.UK**
e:mail: **INFO@CPFC.CO.UK**
tel no: **020 8768 6000**
colours: **BLUE AND RED STRIPED SHIRTS, BLUE SHORTS**
nickname: **THE EAGLES (historically the Glaziers)**
season 2008/09: **CHAMPIONSHIP**

season 07/08: Championship **5TH** p**46** w**18** d**17** l**11** gf**58** ga**42**

After just over a year in the Selhurst Park hot-seat, Peter Taylor was sacked as the manager of the Eagles in early October following a 1-1 draw against former club Hull City which meant that Palace lay in 19th position in the League Championship, just above the drop zone. The club moved quickly to appoint ex-Sheffield United boss Neil Warnock and, under him, the team's position improved dramatically, so much so that by the final game of the season the Eagles were in with a shout of an unlikely place in the Play-Offs. No fewer than four teams were in contention for the final two berths: Palace, Ipswich, Watford and Wolves. Although both Wolves and Ipswich won, their triumphs were insufficient as Palace's 5-0 demolition of Burnley and Watford's draw were sufficient to see the latter two reach the Play-Offs. In the first leg against Bristol City, held at Selhurst Park, Palace lost 2-1 although there was renewed hope when the club took a 1-0 lead at Ashton Gate to force extra time. However, two late goals in extra time saw the Bristol side through. Warnock has had considerable experience in guiding teams at this level and, provided that he manages to retain the core of his team, then Palace must be considered as realistic candidates for the Play-Offs again.

Advance Tickets Tel No: 08712 000071
Fax: 020 8771 5311
Ticket Office/Fax: 020 8653 4708
Training Ground: Copers Cope Road, Beckenham BR3 1RJ

Brief History: Founded 1905. Former Grounds: The Crystal Palace (F.A. Cup Finals venue), London County Athletic Ground (Herne Hill), The Nest (Croydon Common Athletic Ground), moved to Selhurst Park in 1924. Founder members 3rd Division (1920). Record attendance 51,482

(Total) Current Capacity: 23,300 (all seated)
Visiting Supporters' Allocation: Approx 2,000 in Arthur Wait Stand

Nearest Railway Station: Selhurst, Norwood Junction and Thornton Heath

Parking (Car): Street parking and Sainsbury's car park
Parking (Coach/Bus): Thornton Heath
Police Force and Tel No: Metropolitan (020 8653 8568)
Disabled Visitors' Facilities:
Wheelchairs: 56 spaces in Arthur Wait and Holmesdale Stands;
Blind: Commentary available

Anticipated Development(s): Although the club had plans to reconstruct the Main Stand — indeed had Planning Permission for the work — local opposition has meant that no work has been undertaken. Serious thought is now being given to relocation. The long-running split between ownership of the ground and ownership of the club was resolved in October 2006 when Simon Jordan acquired the freehold of Selhurst Park from Ron Noades for £12 million.

65

dagenham and redbridge

London Borough of Barking & Dagenham Stadium, Victoria Road, Dagenham, RM10 7XL

website: **WWW.DAGGERS.CO.UK**
e:mail: **INFO@DAGGERS.CO.UK**
tel no: **020 8592 1549**
colours: **RED AND WHITE SHIRTS, RED SHORTS**
nickname: **THE DAGGERS**
season 2008/09: **LEAGUE TWO**

Promoted from the Conference as Champions in 2006/07, Dagenham & Redbridge under John Still struggled to impose themselves at the higher level and, whilst never in the relegation zone, were sufficiently close to the drop for much of the campaign as to give the club's fans cause for concern. Although by the time that the final match — against already relegated Mansfield — the club's League Two status was assured for another season it's hard to escape the conclusion that 2008/09 will again be a struggle for the Daggers to survive.

Advance Tickets Tel No: 020 8592 1549
Fax: 020 8593 7227
Training Ground: Details omitted at club's request
Brief History: The club has roots in four earlier clubs: Ilford (1881); Leytonstone (1886); Walthamstow Avenue (1900); and Dagenham (1949). Ilford and Leytonstone merged in 1979 and, in 1988, became Redbridge Forest following the incorporation of Walthamstow Athletic. Redbridge Forest moved to Victoria Road in 1991 and formed Dagenham & Redbridge with Dagenham in 1992. Promoted to the Football League at the end of the 2006/07 season. Record attendance (at the Victoria Ground): 7,200; (as Dagenham & Redbridge): 5,949
(Total) Current Capacity: 6,078
Visiting Supporters' Allocation: 1,200 (Pondfield open terrace; all standing)
Nearest Railway Station: Dagenham East (District Line)
Parking (Car): car park at ground or on-street
Parking (Coach/Bus): As directed
Police Force and Tel No: Metropolitan
Disabled Visitors' Facilities:
Wheelchairs: 10 spaces at Pondfield End of Main Stand
Blind: No specific facility

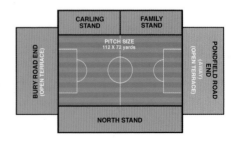

1 A1112 North Rainham Road
2 Dagenham East railway station
3 Oxlow Lane
4 Victoria Road
5 Bury Road
6 Victoria Road
7 North Stand
8 Bury Road Stand
9 Carling Stand
10 Pondfield Road End (away)
11 Family Stand

↑ *North direction (approx)*

◀ 700788
▼ 700790

1 A66
2 To Stockton
3 To A66(M) and A1(M)
4 Neasham Road
5 To Darlington town centre
  and railway station
  (one mile)
6 To Neasham
7 Snipe Lane
8 East Stand (away)

↑ North direction (approx)

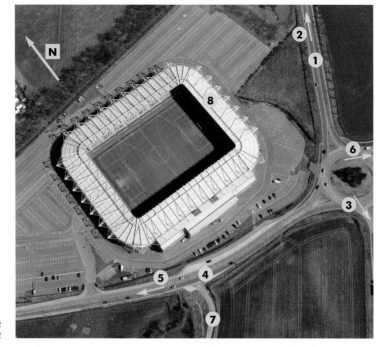

▸ 700522
▾ 700532

darlington

Balfour Webnet Darlington Arena, Neasham Road, Darlington, DL2 1DL

website: **WWW.DARLINGTON–FC.PREMIUMTV.CO.UK**
e:mail: **ENQUIRIES@DARLINGTON–FC.NET**
tel no: **01325 387000**
colours: **WHITE AND BLACK SHIRTS, BLACK SHORTS**
nickname: **THE QUAKERS**
season 2008/09: **LEAGUE TWO**

In Dave Penney's first full season in control of the Quakers, the team prospered in League Two and, whilst never capable of maintaining a serious push for the automatic promotion places, the club cemented its promotion potential by ultimately finishing in sixth place and thus facing Rochdale in the Play-Off semi-final. A 2-1 victory at home gave Darlington the edge, which was added to in the return leg at Spotland. However, two late goals by Rochdale meant that the tie went into extra time. Despite being reduced to 10 men Rochdale held out and were ultimately to prove triumphant in a penalty shoot out. As a result Darlington will again face League Two football in 2008/09 but the team should certainly have the potential to challenge again for a Play-Off place at the very least.

Advance Tickets Tel No: 0870 027 2949
Fax: 01325 387050
Training Ground: Details omitted at Club's request
Brief History: Founded 1883. Founder members of 3rd Division (North) 1921. Relegated from 4th Division 1989. Promoted from GM Vauxhall Conference in 1990. Previous Ground: Feethams; moving to Neasham Road in 2003. Record attendance (at Feethams) 21,023; (at Neasham Road) 11,600
(Total) Current Capacity: 25,000
Visiting Supporters' Allocation: 3,000 in East Stand
Nearest Railway Station: Darlington Bank Top
Parking (Car): Spaces available in adjacent car park (£5.00 fee)
Parking (Coach/Bus): As directed
Police Force and Tel No: Durham (01235 467681)
Disabled Visitors Facilities:
Wheelchairs: 165 places
Blind: No special facility
Anticipated Developments: With the construction of the new ground, there are no further plans for development as the existing ground's capacity is more than adequate for League Two.

season 07/08: League Two **6TH** p**46** w**22** d**12** l**12** gf**67** ga**40**

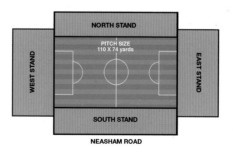

NORTH STAND
PITCH SIZE
110 X 74 yards
WEST STAND
EAST STAND
SOUTH STAND
NEASHAM ROAD

derby county

Pride Park, Derby, Derbyshire, DE24 8XL

website: **WWW.DCFC.CO.UK**
e:mail: **DERBY.COUNTY@DCFC.CO.UK**
tel no: **0871 472 1884**
colours: **WHITE SHIRTS, BLACK SHORTS**
nickname: **THE RAMS**
season 2008/09: **CHAMPIONSHIP**

Having guided the Rams into the Premier League via the Play-Offs at the end of the 2006/07 season, Billy Davies was always on a hiding to nothing at Derby County particularly following the poor start to the season and the appointment of Adam Pearson as new chairman. After just over a year in charge, Davies departed from Pride Park at the end of November with ex-Wigan boss Paul Jewell appointed quickly to the unenviable and almost impossible task of keeping the club in the top flight. Ultimately, however, the task was futile and the club ended up with a number of records for the worst performance in Premier League history — the lowest number of points achieved (11), the quickest relegation, the lowest number of goals scored (20) with the highest goal difference (-69), to name but four — and even the cup competitions failed to offer any relief with Blackpool winning on penalties following a 1-1 draw at Pride Park in the 2nd round of the Carling Cup and Preston North End winning 4-1 at Pride Park in the 4th round of the FA Cup. Although Derby will have the benefit of the parachute payment, much will depend upon Jewell's dealings in the transfer market in the close season as to what sort of campaign the club will have in 2008/09. Many of the players that the club used during the 2007/08 campaign will not be at Pride Park in 2008/09 and Jewell himself recognises that without a significant overhaul of the squad the team could well struggle in the Championship. The club ought to be one of those vying for an automatic spot but it could well be a struggle to achieve a top-half finish without a major injection of confidence.

Advance Tickets Tel No: 0871 472 1884
Fax: 01332 667540
Training Ground: Moor Farm Training Centre, Morley Road, Oakwood, Derby DE21 4TB
Brief History: Founded 1884. Former grounds: The Racecourse Ground, the Baseball Ground (1894-1997), moved to Pride Park 1997. Founder members of the Football League (1888). Record capacity at the Baseball Ground: 41,826; at Pride Park: 33,597
(Total) Current Capacity: 33,597
Visiting Supporters' Allocation: 4,800 maximum in the South Stand
Nearest Railway Station: Derby
Parking (Car): 2,300 places at the ground designated for season ticket holders. Also two 1,000 car parks on the A6/A52 link road. No on-street parking
Parking (Coach/Bus): As directed
Police Force and Tel No: Derbyshire (01332 290100)
Disabled Visitors' Facilities:
Wheelchairs: 70 home/30 away spaces
Blind: Commentary available
Anticipated Development(s): Although formal proposals have yet to be lodged with the planning authorities, the club is planning a £20 million scheme for a hotel, shops and offices adjacent to Pride Park. There are also plans for the expansion of the ground's capacity to 44,000 via the construction of second tiers on the East, North and South stands. Although there was a possibility of this work commencing in the summer of 2008 it's possible that the club's relegation may lead to a rethink.

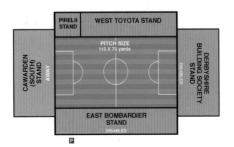

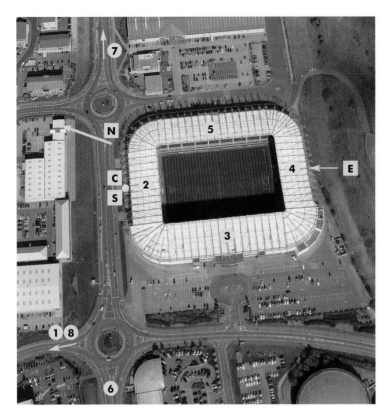

C Club Offices
S Club Shop
E Entrance(s) for visiting
  supporters

1 To Derby Midland BR station
2 North Stand
3 Toyota West Stand
4 South (Cawarden) Stand
  (away)
5 Bombardier East Stand
6 Derwent Parade
7 To A52/M1
8 To City Centre and A6

↑ North direction (approx)

◄ 700534
▼ 700544

1 Lakeside Boulevard
2 To A6182 White Rose Way
3 To Doncaster town centre
and railway station
4 To Junction 3 M18
5 Athletics Stadium
6 Site of 1,000 place car park

↑ North direction (approx)

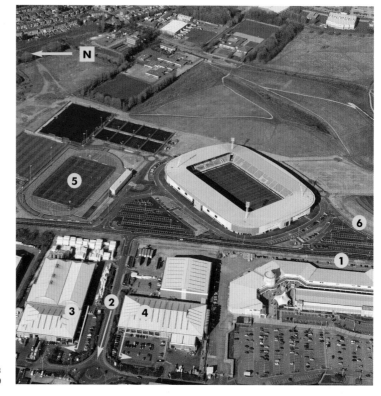

▸ 700553
▾ 700550

doncaster rovers

Keepmoat Stadium, Stadium Way, Lakeside, Doncaster, DN4 5JW

website: **WWW.DONCASTERROVERSFC.PREMIUMTV.CO.UK**
e:mail: **INFO@DONCASTERROVERSFC.CO.UK**
tel no: **01302 764664**
colours: **RED AND WHITE SHIRTS, RED SHORTS**
nickname: **THE ROVERS**
season 2008/09: **LEAGUE ONE**

In the race for automatic promotion right through until the final day of the season, Sean O'Driscoll's Doncaster Rovers were ultimately to achieve the team's third promotion in five years — from the Conference to the Championship — resulting in the team playing in English football's second tier for the first time in 50 years. On the last Saturday, Carlisle, Rovers and Nottingham Forrest all retained an interest in the second automatic promotion place but Doncaster's defeat 2-1 at Cheltenham allied to Carlisle's draw with Bournemouth and Forest's victory over Yeovil meant that Rovers finished third and thus faced the Play-Offs. A 0-0 draw at Roots Hall followed by a 5-1 victory at the Keepmoat Stadium over Southend United meant that the club was heading to Wembley for a Play-Off showdown with Yorkshire rivals Leeds United. Both the League matches between the two teams had been tight affairs and the final was to prove no exception as Rovers ultimately triumphed 1-0. The club's rapid ascent of the pyramid means that the team is the first club to have experienced recent non-league football to reach this level since the rise of Wigan Athletic and so securing Championship status must be the club's priority in 2008/09. The track record of other teams promoted from League One has proved contradictory; some, like Hull, have eventually prospered but others, like Scunthorpe, have made an immediate return to League One. Doncaster will expect a challenge but could have the potential to survive — just.

Advance Tickets Tel No: 01302 762576
Fax: 01302 363525
Training Ground: Cantley Park, Aintree Avenue, Doncaster DN4 6HR
Brief History: Founded 1879. Former grounds: Town Moor, Belle Vue (not later ground), Deaf School Playing field (later name Intake Ground), Bennetthorpe, Belle Vue (1922-2006). Returned to Football League after a five-year absence in 2003. Record attendance (at Belle Vue) 37,149; (at Keepmoat Stadium) 15,001
(Total) Current Capacity: 15,231
Visiting Supporters' Allocation: 3,350 (North Stand)
Nearest Railway Station: Doncaster (two miles)
Parking (Car): 1,000 place car park at ground
Parking (Coach/Bus): As directed
Other Clubs Sharing Ground: Doncaster Dragons RLFC and Doncaster Belles Ladies FC
Police Force and Tel No: South Yorkshire (01302 366744)
Disabled Visitors' Facilities:
Wheelchairs: Three sides of ground (16-18 at pitch side)
Blind: Commentary available
Anticipated Development(s): The club moved into the new Keepmoat Stadium during the course of the 2006/07 season. The ground, which cost £21 million to construct, is owned by Doncaster Council. There are no plans for further development at this stage.

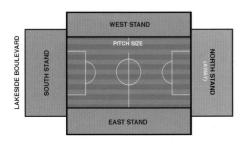

73

everton

Goodison Park, Goodison Road, Liverpool, L4 4EL

website: **WWW.EVERTONFC.COM**
e:mail: **EVERTON@EVERTONFC.COM**
tel no: **0870 442 1878**
colours: **BLUE AND WHITE SHIRTS, WHITE SHORTS**
nickname: **THE TOFFEES**
season 2008/09: **PREMIER LEAGUE**

A season of considerable promise for David Moyes and the Everton squad saw the team emerge as serious contenders for much of the campaign for fourth place — and therefore entry into the Champions League — before Liverpool gradually exerted their dominance to ensure that the 'Big Four' remained exactly that. Thus, as the season drew to a close, Everton were left chasing the all-important fifth place as top of the also-rans, a position which brought with it automatic entry to the UEFA Cup. As the season drew to a close, there were effectively only four teams vying for the position; apart from Everton, there were Portsmouth, Blackburn and Aston Villa. Portsmouth's ambitions seemed to waver once the club had achieved a place in the FA Cup Final whilst Blackburn too failed to sustain a challenge, leaving Villa as the only serious contenders, However, Villa's 2-0 defeat at home by Wigan Athletic left Everton in the driving seat and a 3-1 home victory over Newcastle United allied to Villa's 2-2 draw at Upton Park means that Everton will again feature in Europe in 2008/09. In a season when Premier League teams struggled in domestic cup competitions, Everton was no exception, losing 1-0 at home to Oldham in the 3rd Round of the FA Cup. For 2008/09, Moyes will again be eyeing fourth position in the Premier League as a realistic target, particularly at a time when Liverpool's position is weakened by the ongoing split in the boardroom and uncertainty over the budget for the summer transfer market.

Advance Tickets Tel No: 0870 442 1878
Fax: 0151 286 9112
Training Ground: Bellefield Training Ground, Sandforth Road, West Derby, Liverpool L12 1LW;
Tel: 0151 330 2278;
Fax: 0151 284 5181
Brief History: Founded 1879 as St. Domingo, changed to Everton in 1880. Former grounds: Stanley Park, Priory Road and Anfield (Liverpool F.C. Ground), moved to Goodison Park in 1892. Founder-members Football League (1888). Record attendance 78,299
(Total) Current Capacity: 40,569
Visiting Supporters' Allocation: 3,000 (part of Bullens Road Stand) maximum
Nearest Railway Station: Kirkdale
Parking (Car): Corner of Utting Avenue and Priory Road
Parking (Coach/Bus): Priory Road
Police Force and Tel No: Merseyside (0151 709 6010)
Disabled Visitors' Facilities:
Wheelchairs: Bullens Road Stand
Blind: Commentary available

Anticipated Development(s): Despite opposition — including a local resident who sought permission to demolish the house of Tesco's chairman in revenge, the supermarket chain being a partner in the controversial scheme — the club is progressing its £400 million scheme to construct a new 50,000-seat ground in Knowsley.

C Club Offices
S Club Shop
E Entrance(s) for visiting
  supporters
R Refreshment bars for visiting
  supporters
T Toilets for visiting supporters

1 A580 Walton Road
2 Bullen Road
3 Goodison Road
4 Car Park
5 Liverpool Lime Street BR
  Station (2 miles)
6 To M57 Junction 2,
  4 and 5
7 Stanley Park
8 Bullens Road Stand
9 Park Stand
10 Main Stand
11 Gwladys Stand

↑ North direction (approx)

◄ 700047
▼ 700053

▸ 701389
▾ 701381

exeter city

St James Park, Stadium Way, Exeter, EX4 6PX

website: **WWW.EXETERCITYFC.PREMIUMTV.CO.UK**
e:mail: **ENQUIRIES@EXETERCITYFC.CO.UK**
tel no: **0871 855 1904**
colours: **RED AND WHITE SHIRTS, BLACK SHORTS**
nickname: **THE GRECIANS**
season 2008/09: **LEAGUE TWO**

After some five years outside the Football League, the Grecians reclaimed their League spot in the most dramatic of ways having lost out in the Play-Off final in 2006/07. One of a number of teams competing for the Play-Off places, Paul Tisdale's team ultimately finished in fourth place and thus faced local rivals Torquay United in the Play-Off semi-final. A 2-1 away win for United at St James Park gave Torquay the edge, which was increased by the addition of a third at Plainmoor; with some 20min remaining and with Torquay leading 3-1 on aggregate all looked lost for City. However, four late goals gave City a dramatic victory with the result that the Grecians faced another ex-League team, Cambridge United, at Wembley. In 2008 there was to be no repeat of the disappointment of 2007 as a single first half goal brought victory to the Devon side. Teams promoted through the Play-Offs have often struggled and for City, the club's first priority must be to consolidate its position back in the League. The team should be capable of achieving this.

Telephone: 0871 855 1904
Advance Tickets Tel No: 0871 855 1904
Fax: 01392 413959
Web Site: www.exetercityfc.premiumtv.co.uk
E-mail: enquiries@exetercityfc.co.uk
Training Ground: Cat & Fiddle Training Ground, Sidmouth Road, Clyst St Mary, Exeter EX5 1DP
Brief History: Founded in 1904 as a result of the amalgamation of St Sidwell United and Exeter United. Founder members of Third Division (1920). Relegated to Conference 2003; League status reclaimed 2008
(Total) Current Capacity: 9,036 (3,806 seated)
Visiting Supporters' Allocation:, 1,200 (St James' Road End — open terrace) plus limited seats in Flybe Stand. If limited away support is anticipated, then the Flybe Stand accommodation only is used.
Club Colours: Red and white shirts, black shorts
Nearest Railway Station: Exeter St James Park
Parking (Car): National Car park or council car parks (no on-street parking; residents' only scheme in operation)
Parking (Coach/Bus): Paris Street bus station
Police Force and Tel No: Devon & Cornwall (08452 777444)
Disabled Visitors' Facilities:
Wheelchairs: c40 places in Flybe Stand and Big Bank
Blind: No special facility.

FLYBE STAND
AWAY
PITCH SIZE
114 X 73 yards
BIG BANK
ST. JAMES ROAD
(OPEN TERRACE)
AWAY
GRANDSTAND

fulham

Craven Cottage, Stevenage Road, Fulham, London. SW6 6HH

website: **WWW.FULHAMFC.COM**
e:mail: **ENQUIRIES@FULHAMFC.COM**
tel no: **0870 442 1222**
colours: **WHITE SHIRTS, BLACK SHORTS**
nickname: **THE COTTAGERS**
season 2008/09: **PREMIER LEAGUE**

An early shock for the festive season saw Lawrie Sanchez dismissed as Fulham boss just before Christmas following a dismal run of form that had seen the Cottagers drift into the relegation zone. Although Sanchez had succeeded in keeping Fulham in the Premier League at the end of the 2006/07 season and had been given significant funds during the close season, a record of only two wins was considered dire. Ray Lewington was, once again, appointed as caretaker manager before the experienced and well-travelled Roy Hodgson was given the task of keeping Fulham in the Premier League. For much of the second half of the campaign it looked as though Fulham were doomed, particularly as the club struggled to gain anything away from home. However, with the club rooted in the relegation zone, a dramatic reversal of fortunes in the match at Manchester City saw the Cottagers turn a 2-0 deficit into a 3-2 victory, sparking a revival that saw the team also defeat fellow strugglers Birmingham City to ensure that, on the final Sunday, provided that Fulham equalled or bettered the results of the games involving Reading and Birmingham, then Premier League football was again assured at Craven Cottage. With both of the two potential relegation candidates running riot, Fulham left it late to score a 1-0 win away at Portsmouth, with Danny Murphy proving to be an unlikely hero. Thus Mohamed Al-Fayed's Fulham survives in the top flight again and, with potentially weaker teams coming up from the Championship, the club should probably be able to ensure survival again at the end of 2008/09 with more ease than in 2007/08.

Club Offices: Fulham FC Training Ground, Motspur Park, New Malden, Surrey KT3 6PT
Advance Tickets Tel No: 0870 442 1234
Fax: 020 8442 0236
Training Ground: The Academy, Fulham FC, Motspur Park, New Malden, Surrey, KT3 6PT; Tel: 020 8336 7430
Brief History: Founded in 1879 at St. Andrews Fulham, changed name to Fulham in 1898. Former grounds: Star Road, Ranelagh Club, Lillie Road, Eel Brook Common, Purer's Cross, Barn Elms, Half Moon (Wasps Rugby Football Ground), Craven Cottage (from 1894), moved to Loftus Road 2002 and returned to Craven Cottage for start of the 2004/05 season.
Record Attendance: Craven Cottage (49,335)
(Total) Current Capacity: 26,300
Visiting Supporters' Allocation: 3,000 in Putney End
Nearest Railway Station: Putney Bridge (Tube)
Parking (Car): Street parking
Parking(Coach/Bus): Stevenage Road
Police Force and Tel No: Metropolitan (020 7741 6212)
Disabled Visitors' Facilities:
Wheelchairs: Main Stand and Hammersmith End
Blind: No special facility
Anticipated Development(s): It was announced in early October 2007 that the club was looking to increase Craven Cottage's capacity by some 4,000 by infilling the corners between the corners of the existing stands.

◄ 700230
▼ 700228

E Entrance(s) for visiting
supporters
R Refreshment bars for visiting
supporters
T Toilets for visiting supporters

1 River Thames
2 Stevenage Road
3 Finlay Street
4 Putney Bridge Tube Station
(0.5 mile)
5 Putney End (away)
6 Riverside Stand
7 Main Stand
8 Hammersmith End
9 Craven Cottage

↑ *North direction (approx)*

E Entrance(s) for visiting
 supporters

1 Redfern Avenue
2 Toronto Road
3 Gordon Road
4 Gillingham BR station
 (¼ mile)
5 Gordon Street Stand
6 New two-tier Main
 (Medway) Stand
7 New Rainham End Stand
8 Gillingham End; uncovered
 seating (away)

↑ *North direction (approx)*

▸ 700771
▾ 700780

gillingham

KRBS Priestfield Stadium, Redfern Avenue, Gillingham, Kent, ME7 4DD

website: **WWW.GILLINGHAM FOOTBALLCLUB.PREMIUMTV.CO.UK**
e:mail: **INFO@PRIESTFIELD.COM**
tel no: **01634 300000**
colours: **BLUE AND BLACK HOOPED SHIRTS, BLUE SHORTS**
nickname: **THE GILLS**
season 2008/09: **LEAGUE TWO**

After a run of five league defeats in the first six matches of the season, Ronnie Jepson resigned as Gillingham manager in early September. He was replaced in early November by Mark Stimson, who came to the club from Conference outfit Stevenage Borough. Under Stimson, the club was involved in the battle to avoid the drop throughout the season, although it was not until the final day that the club's ultimate fortune was settled. One of four teams — the others being Bournemouth, Cheltenham and Crewe — that could fill the final two relegation spots, Gillingham needed a victory at high-flying Leeds United and hope that other teams slipped up. In the event, although Bournemouth drew, Gillingham's narrow defeat at Elland Road was irrelevant as Cheltenham's 2-1 victory over Doncaster Rovers was sufficient to consign Gillingham to League Two irrespective of events in West Yorkshire. As a relegated team, Gillingham ought to be one of the favourites to make a bid for the Play-Offs at least.

Advance Tickets Tel No: 01634 300000
Fax: 01634 850986
Training Ground: Beechings Cross, Grange Road, Gillingham ME7 2UD
Brief History: Founded 1893, as New Brompton, changed name to Gillingham in 1913. Founder-members Third Division (1920). Lost Football League status (1938), re-elected to Third Division South (1950). Record attendance 23,002
(Total) Current Capacity: 11,582 (all Seated)
Visiting Supporters' Allocation: 1,500 (in Gillingham (Brian Moore Stand) End)
Nearest Railway Station: Gillingham
Parking (Car): Street parking
Parking (Coach/Bus): As directed by Police
Police Force and Tel No: Kent (01634 234488)
Disabled Visitors' Facilities:
Wheelchairs: Redfern Avenue (Main) Stand
Blind: No special facility

Anticipated Development(s): The old open Town End Terrace was demolished during 2003 and replaced by a new temporary open stand. Planning Permission was granted in 2003 for the construction of a new 3,500-seat stand, to be named after noted fan the late Brian Moore, although work has yet to commence. Despite the investment at Priestfield, however, the club is investigating, in conjunction with the local council, the possibility of constructing a new stadium at Temple Marsh. Towards the end of January, chairman Paul Scally announced that he hoped to make a statement about relocation within six weeks with a view to the club moving to a new site within the Medway area for the start of the 2010/11 season.

season 07/08: League One **22ND** (relegated) p**46** w**11** d**13** l**22** gf**44** ga**73**

grimsby town

Blundell Park, Cleethorpes, DN35 7PY

website: **WWW.GRIMSBY–TOWNFC.PREMIUMTV.CO.UK**
e:mail: **ENQUIRIES@GTFC.CO.UK**
tel no: **01472 605050**
colours: **BLACK AND WHITE STRIPED SHIRTS, BLACK SHORTS**
nickname: **THE MARINERS**
season 2008/09: **LEAGUE TWO**

Under Stuart Watkiss Town had a relatively disappointing season, ultimately finishing in 16th place as one of the teams that was never strong enough to mount a sustained challenge for the Play-Offs nor weak enough to be dragged into the relegation battle. Outside the League, the club did achieve one considerable success in cup competitions, with a 1-0 victory over promotion chasing League One outfit Carlisle United in the 1st round of the FA Cup at Blundell Park. For 2008/09 fans will be expecting a much improved League performance from the Mariners and the team should be amongst those vying for a top-half finish at least.

Advance Tickets Tel No: 01472 605050
Fax: 01472 693665
Training Ground: Cheapside, Waltham, Grimsby
Brief History: Founded in 1878, as Grimsby Pelham, changed name to Grimsby Town in 1879. Former Grounds: Clee Park (two adjacent fields) and Abbey Park, moved to Blundell Park in 1899. Founder-members 2nd Division (1892). Record attendance 31,651
(Total) Current Capacity: 9,546 (all seated)
(Total) Current Capacity: 9,546 (All seated)
Visiting Supporters' Allocation: 2,000 in Osmond Stand
Club Colours: Black and white striped shirts, black shorts
Nearest Railway Station: Cleethorpes
Parking (Car): Street parking
Parking (Coach/Bus): Harrington Street
Police Force and Tel No: Humberside (01472 359171)
Disabled Visitors' Facilities:
Wheelchairs: Harrington Street (Main) Stand
Blind: Commentary available

Anticipated Development(s): In late January 2006 it was announced that the club had applied for planning permission to construct a new 20,100-seat ground, to be called the ConocoPhillips Stadium, at Great Coates. Outline planning permission for the work was granted in early 2007. The cost, some £14.4 million, includes a £10 million retail park, with the first phase providing a 12,000-seat facility. Planning permission was granted in December 2007.

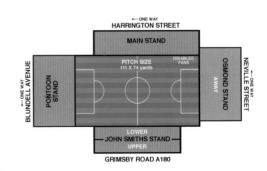

C Club Offices
S Club Shop
E Entrance(s) for visiting supporters
R Refreshment bars for visiting supporters
T Toilets for visiting supporters

1 A180 Grimsby Road
2 Cleethorpes BR Station (1½ miles)
3 To Grimsby and M180 Junction 5
4 Harrington Street
5 Constitutional Avenue
6 Humber Estuary

⬆ North direction (approx)

◄ 697766
▼ 697756

C Club Offices
S Club Shop
E Entrance(s) for visiting supporters

1 A179 Clarence Road
2 To Hartlepool Church Street BR Station
3 To Marina Way
4 Site of former Greyhound Stadium
5 To Middlesbrough A689 & A1(M)
6 To A19 North
7 Rink End Stand

⬆ *North direction (approx)*

▸ 700556
▾ 700565

hartlepool united

Victoria Park, Clarence Road, Hartlepool, TS24 8BZ

website: **WWW.HARTLEPOOLUNITED.PREMIUMTV.CO.UK**
e:mail: **ENQUIRIES@HARTLEPOOLUNITED.CO.UK**
tel no: **01429 272584**
colours: **BLUE AND WHITE STRIPED SHIRTS, BLUE SHORTS**
nickname: **THE POOL**
season 2008/09: **LEAGUE ONE**

Promoted at the end of the 2006/07 season, the first priority for Danny Wilson and his team was to ensure League One survival and, in this aspiration, the club was successful, ultimately finishing in a position of creditable mid-table security. Apart from the League, the club also had limited success in the Carling Cup, defeating Championship strugglers Scunthorpe United 2-1 at Glanford Park in the 1st round but less in the FA Cup where League Two promotion hopefuls Hereford United proved victorious 2-0 in the 2nd round match at Edgar Street. Ironically, the club will again meet both teams, but in League fixtures, in 2008/09. Now established in League One, Wilson's pedigree should ensure that the club continues to make progress, although a top-half finish is perhaps the best that can be expected.

Advance Tickets Tel No: 01429 272584
Fax: 01429 863007
Training Ground: Details omitted at club's request
Brief History: Founded 1908 as Hartlepools United, changed to Hartlepool (1968) and to Hartlepool United in 1977. Founder-members 3rd Division (1921). Record attendance 17,426
(Total) Current Capacity: 7,629 (3,966)
Visiting Supporters' Allocation: 1,000 (located in Rink Stand)
Nearest Railway Station: Hartlepool Church Street
Parking (Car): Street parking and rear of clock garage
Parking (Coach/Bus): As directed
Police Force and Tel No: Cleveland (01429 221151
Disabled Visitors' Facilities:
Wheelchairs: Cyril Knowles Stand and Rink End
Blind: Commentary available
Anticipated Development(s): The plans for the redevelopment of the Millhouse Stand are still progressing, although there is now no definite timescale. When this work does commence, the ground's capacity will be reduced to 5,000 temporarily.

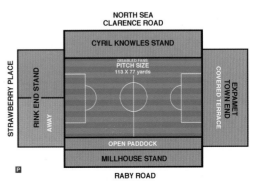

NORTH SEA
CLARENCE ROAD

CYRIL KNOWLES STAND

STRAWBERRY PLACE

RINK END STAND

AWAY

DISABLED FANS
PITCH SIZE
113 X 77 yards

OPEN PADDOCK

MILLHOUSE STAND

EXPAMET
TOWN END
COVERED TERRACE

RABY ROAD

P

hereford united

Edgar Street, Hereford, HR4 9JU

website: **WWW.HEREFORDUNITED.CO.UK**
e:mail: **HUFC1939@HOTMAIL.COM**
tel no: **01432 276666**
colours: **WHITE SHIRTS, WHITE SHORTS**
nickname: **THE BULLS**
season 2008/09: **LEAGUE ONE**

season 07/08: League Two **3RD** (promoted) p**46** w**26** d**10** l**10** gf**72** ga**41**

Promoted from the Conference at the end of the 2005/06 season, Graham Turner's Hereford side — and it is very much his team as he owns it as well as managing it — proved to be the League Two surprise package in its second season back in the League as the Bulls stormed up the table to be one of the teams challenging for automatic promotion. Promotion was achieved on the penultimate Saturday of the season, bringing League One football to Edgar Street. Away from the League, United also reminded fans of the club's long tradition of heroics in the cup. In the FA Cup, having been drawn against League One Leeds United in the 1st round of the FA Cup at Edgar Street, the fans must have thought that the club's chances had disappeared following the home draw; clearly, however, the players thought differently as they achieved an impressive 1-0 victory at Elland Road in the replay. A further success saw the team defeat another League One opponent — Tranmere Rovers — in the 3rd round at Edgar Street. Ironically, both of these teams will again face the Bulls in 2008/09, but in League fixtures this time. It is often the case that clubs struggle after two promotions in quick succession and it may well be that United struggle to retain their newly-acquired status but Turner certainly has the experience to maximise the team's potential.

Advance Tickets Tel No: 01432 276666
Fax: 01432 341359
Training Ground: details omitted at club's request
Brief History: Founded 1924; first elected to the Football League 1972; relegated to the Conference 1997; promoted through the Play-Offs at the end of 2005/06. Record attendance 18,115
(Total) Current Capacity: 8,843 (1,761 seated)
Visiting Supporters' Allocation: tbc (Floors 2 Go [Edgar Street] Stand and Blackfriars Street End)
Nearest Railway Station: Hereford
Parking (Car): Merton Meadow and Edgar Street
Parking (Coach/Bus): Cattle Market
Police Force and Tel No: West Mercia (08457 444888)
Disabled Visitors' Facilities:
Wheelchairs: Edgar Street (limited)
Blind: Commentary available

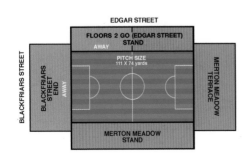

C Club Offices
S Club Shop
E Entrance(s) for visiting
  supporters
R Refreshment bars for visiting
  supporters
T Toilets for visiting supporters

1 A49(T) Edgar Street
2 Blackfriars Street
3 Len Weston Stand
4 Merton Meadow Stand
5 Merton Meadow Terrace
6 Blackfriars Street End
7 To Town Centre and
  Hereford BR Station

↑ North direction (approx)

◄ 700427
▼ 700436

▲ 700085
▸ 700079

C Club Offices
S Club Shop
E Entrance(s) for visiting
   supporters

1 To Leeds and M62
   Junction 25
2 A62 Leeds Road
3 To Huddersfield BR station
   (1¼ miles)
4 Disabled parking
5 North Stand
6 St Andrews pay car park
7 Coach park
8 South (Pink Link) Stand
   (away)

↑ North direction (approx)

huddersfield town

The Galpharm Stadium, Leeds Road, Huddersfield, HD1 6PX

website: **WWW.HTAFC.PREMIUMTV.CO.UK**
e:mail: **INFO@HTAFC.COM**
tel no: **0870 444 4677**
colours: **BLUE AND WHITE STRIPED SHIRTS, WHITE SHORTS**
nickname: **THE TERRIERS**
season 2008/09: **LEAGUE ONE**

Appointed in April 2007, Andy Ritchie lasted less than a year in charge of Huddersfield Town, being sacked on 1 April following a 4-1 defeat away at Oldham Athletic, a result that left Town in 14th place some 10 points off the pace of even the Play-Offs. The club moved swiftly to appoint Gerry Murphy as caretaker before bringing in the experienced Stan Ternent to the club later in the month. Under the new boss and his assistant Ronnie Jepson the team slightly improved its League position — ultimately finishing in 10th place — although the difference in points between the club and the final Play-Off place remained an infuriating 10. An ambitious club, Huddersfield should have the potential to make a decent bid for the Play-Offs a least and, in Ternent, a boss who's capable of creating a successful team. Anything other than a good start to the season could see the knives out at the Galpharm Stadium again, however.

Advance Tickets Tel No: 0870 444 4552
Fax: 01484 484101
Training Ground: Storthes Hall, Storthes Hall Lane, Kirkburton, Huddersfield HD8 0WA
Brief History: Founded 1908, elected to Football League in 1910. First Club to win the Football League Championship three years in succession. Moved from Leeds Road ground to Kirklees (Alfred McAlpine) Stadium 1994/95 season. Record attendance (Leeds Road) 67,037; Galpharm Stadium: 23,678
(Total) Current Capacity: 24,500
Visiting Supporters' Allocation: 4,037 (all seated)
Nearest Railway Station: Huddersfield
Parking (Car): Car parks (pre-sold) adjacent to ground
Parking (Coach/Bus): Car parks adjacent to ground
Other Clubs Sharing Ground: Huddersfield Giants RLFC
Police Force and Tel No: West Yorkshire (01484 422122)
Disabled Visitors' Facilities:
Wheelchairs: Three sides of Ground, at low levels and raised area, including toilet access
Blind: Area for partially sighted with Hospital Radio commentary
Anticipated Development(s): With completion of the new North Stand, work on the Galpharm Stadium is over.

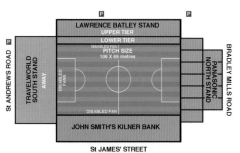

hull city

Kingston Communication Stadium, Walton Street, Hull, East Yorkshire, HU3 6HU

website: **WWW.HULLCITYAFC.PREMIUMTV.CO.UK**
e:mail: **INFO@HULLTIGERS.COM**
tel no: **0870 837 0003**
colours: **AMBER SHIRTS, BLACK SHORTS**
nickname: **THE TIGERS**
season 2008/09: **PREMIER LEAGUE**

One of the least wanted of all footballing records — that Hull was the largest city in Europe never to have had a team playing in its native top flight — was finally laid to rest at the end of the season when Phil Brown's team triumphed in a 1-0 victory in the League Championship Play-Off Final at Wembley. One of the dark horses in the Championship campaign, City's promotion challenge built as the year wore on and, even on the final Sunday, the Tigers were still in with a realistic chance of automatic promotion. Needing to win in order to stand a chance of overtaking Stoke on the final day, a 1-0 defeat at Play-Off chasing Ipswich Town allied to Stoke's 0-0 draw with Leicester City meant that the team finished in third place. A 1-0 victory over sixth-placed Watford at Vicarage Road gave City the edge, which was comprehensively extended courtesy of a 5-1 home win to set up a decider with Bristol City at Wembley. Veteran striker Dean Windass's first half goal was enough to send Hull into the top flight for the first time in more than a century. Although promotion represents a financial bonanza — some £60 million, it's estimated — it's hard to escape the conclusion that City will struggle to make an impact and the most that fans can hope for is that they enjoy themselves at this level and endeavour to exceed the meagre total of points obtained by the last club — Derby County — to be promoted through the Play-Offs.

Advance Tickets Tel No: 0870 837 0004
Fax: 01482 304882
Training Ground: Millhouse Woods Lane, Cottingham, Kingston upon Hull HU16 4HB
Brief History: Founded 1904. Former grounds: The Boulevard (Hull Rugby League Ground), Dairycoates, Anlaby Road Cricket Circle (Hull Cricket Ground), Anlaby Road, Boothferry Park (from 1946). Moved to Kingston Communications Stadium in late 2002. Record attendance (at Boothferry Park) 55,019; (at Kingston Communications Stadium) 25,280
(Total) Current Capacity: 25,504
Visiting Supporters' Allocation: 4,000 all-seated in North Stand
Nearest Railway Station: Hull Paragon
Parking (Car): There are 1,800 spaces on the Walton Street Fairground for use on match days
Parking (Coach/Bus): As directed
Other Clubs Sharing Ground: Hull RLFC
Police Force and Tel No: Humberside (01482 220148)
Disabled Visitors' facilities:
Wheelchairs: c300 places
Blind: Contact club for details
Anticipated Development(s): The club moved into the new Kingston Communication Stadium towards the end of 2002. The ground is shared with Hull RLFC. The total cost of the 25,504-seat ground was £44million. The West Stand is provided with two tiers and there are plans for the construction of a second tier on the East and South Stands, taking the capacity to 34,000 if required.

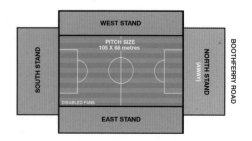

1 A1105 Anlaby Road
2 Arnold Lane
3 West Stand
4 East Stand
5 Walton Street
6 To city centre and railway station
7 Car parks
8 Railway line towards Scarborough
9 Railway line towards Leeds
10 A1105 westwards towards A63 and M62

↑ North direction (approx)

◄ 700568
▼ 700578

C Club Offices
E Entrance(s) for visiting supporters
R Refreshment bars for visiting supporters
T Toilets for visiting supporters

1 A137 West End Road
2 Sir Alf Ramsay Way
3 Portman Road
4 Princes Street
5 To Ipswich BR Station
6 Car Parks
7 Cobbold Stand
8 Britannia Stand
9 North Stand
10 Greene King (South) Stand

↑ *North direction (approx)*

▸ 699778
▾ 699784

ipswich town

Portman Road, Ipswich, IP1 2DA

website: **WWW.ITFC.PREMIUMTV.CO.UK**
e:mail: **ENQUIRIES@ITFC.CO.UK**
tel no: **01473 400500**
colours: **BLUE SHIRTS, WHITE SHORTS**
nickname: **THE TRACTORBOYS**
season 2008/09: **CHAMPIONSHIP**

A season of some progress at Portman Road saw Jim Magilton's side improve considerably on the position of mid-table mediocrity achieved at the end of the 2006/07 season. One of a pack of teams chasing the final Play-Off places on the last Sunday of the season, Town — along with Crystal Palace, Watford and Wolves — were all vying for the final two spots. Although Town were eighth at the start of the day's play, the club's superior goal difference would give them the edge over both Wolves at Watford if results went in Town's favour. Unfortunately, however, despite a 1-0 victory over Hull City at Portman Road — a result that helped ensure Stoke City's promotion — Wolves' victory over Plymouth and Watford's draw with Blackpool meant that Town remained in eighth place thus ensuring Championship football again. With the battle to achieve promotion from the Championship getting harder season by season, it's hard to escape the conclusion that Town's prospects for 2008/09 are perhaps the Play-Offs at best.

Advance Tickets Tel No: 0870 1110555
Fax: 01473 400040
Training Ground: Ipswich Town Academy, Playford Road, Rushmere, Ipswich IP4 5RU
Brief History: Founded 1887 as Ipswich Association F.C., changed to Ipswich Town in 1888. Former Grounds: Broom Hill & Brookes Hall, moved to Portman Road in 1888. Record attendance 38,010
(Total) Current Capacity: 30,311
Visiting Supporters' Allocation: 1,700 all seated in Cobbold Stand
Nearest Railway Station: Ipswich
Parking (Car): Portman Road, Portman Walk & West End Road
Parking (Coach/Bus): West End Road
Police Force and Tel No: Suffolk (01473 611611)
Disabled Visitors' Facilities:
Wheelchairs: Lower Britannia Stand
Blind: Commentary available
Anticipated Development(s): The new Greene King (South) Stand has been followed by the construction of the new two-tier, 7,035-seat, North Stand, which was initially delayed as a result of legal action. The completion of the two stands takes Portman Road's capacity to more than 30,000.

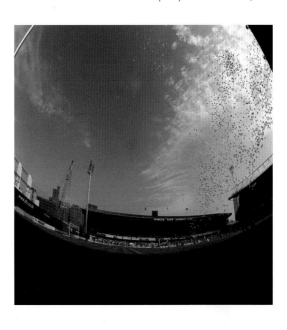

leeds united

Elland Road, Leeds, LS11 0ES

website: **WWW.LEEDSUNITED.COM**
e:mail: **RECEPTION@LEEDSUNITED.COM**
tel no: **0113 367 6000**
colours: **WHITE SHIRTS, WHITE SHORTS**
nickname: **UNITED**
season 2008/09: **LEAGUE ONE**

Having been docked 10 points at the end of the 2006/07 season for going into Administration, Leeds United were penalised a further 15 points before the start of the League One campaign as a result of problems with the process of Administration. However, the team's early season form was such that this handicap was soon removed as the team rapidly closed towards the top of the table. However, the departure of coach Gus Poyet to Spurs seems to have led to a decline in form and the break-up of the management team was further compounded by the departure of Dennis Wise at the end of January to join Kevin Keegan at Newcastle United. The club moved quickly in appointing ex-player and experienced manager Gary McAllister as the new boss and under him the team cemented its place in the Play-Offs. Frustratingly for the Elland Road faithful, an appeal against the 15-point deduction was rejected — the team would have made an automatic promotion place had the points been restored — and so faced Carlisle United in the Play-Offs. A 2-1 victory at Elland Road seemed to give the Cumbrian side the edge but a 2-0 victory at Brunton Park sent Leeds United through and set up a Wembley final against Doncaster Rovers. As in 2005/06, however, Leeds failed to achieve victory in a Play-Off final, losing this time 1-0 in a tightly fought match. Away from the League, United suffered the embarrassment of a first round FA Cup 1-0 defeat at Elland Road in a replay against League Two Hereford United. Ironically, United's failure to achieve promotion means that Hereford will be amongst teams that Leeds will face during the 2008/09 season. Undoubtedly, with the imbalance caused by the 15-point deduction behind them Leeds will be amongst the pre-season favourites to grab one of the automatic promotion places; anything less than a play-Off place is unlikely.

Advance Tickets Tel No: 0871 334 1992
Fax: 0113 367 6050
Training Ground: Thorp Arch, Walton Road, Nr Wetherby LS23 7BA
Brief History: Founded 1919, formed from the former 'Leeds City' Club, who were disbanded following expulsion from the Football League in October 1919. Joined Football League in 1920. Record attendance 57,892
(Total) Current Capacity: 40,296
Visiting Supporters' Allocation: 1,725 in South East Corner (can be increased to 3,662 in South Stand if necessary)
Nearest Railway Station: Leeds City
Parking (Car): Car parks adjacent to ground
Parking (Coach/Bus): As directed by Police
Police Force and Tel No: West Yorkshire (0113 243 5353)
Disabled Visitors' Facilities:
Wheelchairs: West Stand and South Stand
Blind: Commentary available
Anticipated Development(s): The club has plans for the development of land surrounding Elland Road to include a concert hall and large car park. There is, however, no timescale for this work.

*15 points deducted as a result of the previous season's Administration

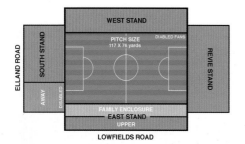

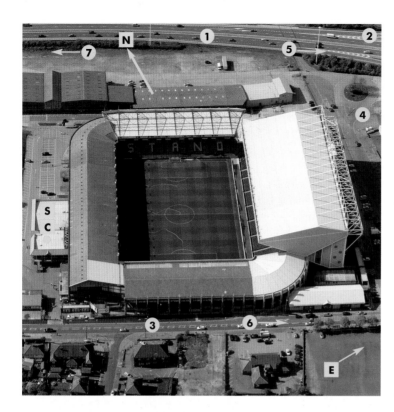

C Club Offices
S Club Shop
E Entrance(s) for visiting
  supporters

1 M621
2 M621 Junction 2
3 A643 Elland Road
4 Lowfields Road
5 To A58
6 City Centre and BR station
7 To M62 and M1

↑ North direction (approx)

◄ 700145
▼ 700135

C Club Offices

1 Raw Dykes Road
2 Eastern Road
3 A426 Aylestone Road
4 To Lutterworth
5 To city centre and railway station (one mile)
6 Burnmoor Street
7 River Soar

↑ *North direction (approx)*

▸ 699793
▾ 699804

leicester city

Walkers Stadium, Filbert Road, Leicester, LE2 7FL

website: **WWW.LCFC.PREMIUMTV.CO.UK**
e:mail: **TICKET.SALES@LCFC.CO.UK**
tel no: **0844 815 6000**
colours: **BLUE SHIRTS, WHITE SHORTS**
nickname: **THE FOXES**
season 2008/09: **LEAGUE ONE**

In late August, after only three months and a handful of games in charge, Martin Allen left City by mutual consent following a breakdown in relations between him and chairman Milan Mandaric. The club moved quickly, appointing the ex-Nottingham Forest boss, Gary Megson, who had been out of management since leaving the City Ground in February 2006, shortly before the home game with QPR in mid-September. Megson's sojourn at the Walkers Stadium was, however, destined to be short-lived as, working without a contract, he departed on 24 October to take over as the new manager at Bolton. With Megson's departure, Frank Burrows and Gerry Taggart were appointed joint caretaker managers. The club moved quickly to appoint ex-Plymouth boss Ian Holloway to the vacant position. Under Holloway the club's position deteriorated markedly as the Foxes slipped towards the drop zone and City was one of five teams — the others being Blackpool, Southampton, Sheffield Wednesday and Coventry — that mathematically faced the drop to League One. Although Coventry did their best to assist the Foxes' survival bid, being trounced 4-1 at Charlton, results at Blackpool, Sheffield Wednesday and Southampton meant that Leicester's draw at the Britannia Stadium saw the Foxes relegated. The final match was one of mixed emotions for the fans at the game; a single point was sufficient to ensure that Stoke were promoted but not enough to maintain Leicester's Championship status. Shortly after the end of the season it was announced that Holloway was departing the Walkers Stadium, to be replaced by Nigel Pearson. Thus the new season will open with Pearson's team facing Hereford United rather than Birmingham City; as a relegated team the Foxes should have the potential to make a serious bid for automatic promotion but as other fallen giants, such as Nottingham Forest and Leeds United have discovered, football at this level is no respecter of traditional 'big' teams.

Advance Tickets Tel No: 0844 815 5000
Fax: 0116 247 0585
Brief History: Founded 1884 as Leicester Fosse, changed name to Leicester City in 1919. Former grounds: Fosse Road South, Victoria Road, Belgrave Cycle Track, Mill Lane, Aylstone Road Cricket Ground and Filbert Street (from 1891). The club moved to the new Walkers Stadium for the start of the 2002/03 season. Record attendance (at Filbert Street) 47,298; (at Walkers Stadium) 32,148
(Total) Current Capacity: 32,500 (all seated)
Visiting Supporters' Allocation: 3,000 (all seated) in North East of Ground
Nearest Railway Station: Leicester
Parking (Car): NCP car park
Parking (Coach/Bus): As directed
Police Force and Tel No: Leicester (0116 222 2222)
Disabled Visitors Facilities:
Wheelchairs:186 spaces spread through all stands
Blind: Match commentary via hospital radio
Anticipated Developments: The club moved into the new 32,500-seat Walkers Stadium at the start of the 2002/03 season. Although there are no plans at present, the stadium design allows for the construction of a second tier to the East Stand, taking capacity to 40,000.

season 07/08: Championship **22ND** (relegated) p46 w12 d16 l18 gf42 ga45

leyton orient

Matchroom Stadium, Brisbane Road, Leyton, ondon, E10 5NF

website: **WWW.LEYTONORIENT.PREMIUMTV.CO.UK**
e:mail: **INFO@LEYTONORIENT.NET**
tel no: **0871 310 1881**
colours: **RED SHIRTS, RED SHORTS**
nickname: **THE O'S**
season 2008/09: **LEAGUE ONE**

season 07/08: League One **14TH** p**46** w**16** d**12** l**18** gf**49** ga**63**

Ultimately a somewhat disappointing season for Martin Ling's team — albeit lacking the drama of the previous campaign's battle against relegation — initially saw Orient as one of the teams in the hunt for a Play-Off place but as the season drew on the team gradually drifted down the table ultimately to finish in a position of mid-table mediocrity. Away from the League, the club did have one notable victory in the 1st round of the Carling Cup — a 2-1 win at Loftus Road against Championship side QPR. For the new season, the club's status as a League One outfit seems to be reasonably well cemented and the team should perhaps have the potential to make a more sustained bid for the Play-Offs, although a top-half finish is perhaps the best that can be hoped for.

Advance Tickets Tel No: 0871 310 1883
Fax: 0871 310 1882
Training Ground: Southgate Hockey Centre, Trent Park, Snakes Lane, Barnet EN4 0PS
Brief History: Founded 1887 as Clapton Orient, from Eagle Cricket Club (formerly Glyn Cricket Club formed in 1881). Changed name to Leyton Orient (1946), Orient, (1966), Leyton Orient (1987). Former grounds: Glyn Road, Whittles Athletic Ground, Millfields Road, Lea Bridge Road, Wembley Stadium (2 games), moved to Brisbane Road in 1937. Record attendance 34,345

(Total) Current Capacity: 9,271 (all seated)
Visiting Supporters' Allocation: 1,000 (all seated) in East Stand/Terrace
Nearest Railway Station: Leyton (tube), Leyton Midland Road
Parking (Car): Street parking
Parking (Coach/Bus): As directed by Police
Police Force and Tel No: Metropolitan (020 8556 8855)
Disabled Visitors' Facilities:
Wheelchairs: Windsor Road
Blind: Match commentary supplied on request
Anticipated Development(s): Work was scheduled to start on the North Stand towards the end of October 2006 and the new 1,351-seat structure was completed by the end of the 2006/07 season. In the summer of 2007 plans for the 2012 Olympic Stadium were announced. A permanent capacity of 25,000 is anticipated with a temporary upper tier offering a total capacity of 80,000 for the duration of the Games. There is a possibility, given that no post-2012 use has as yet been identified for the stadium, that Leyton Orient may relocate to the ground for the start of the 2013/14 season.

C Club Offices
S Club Shop
E Entrance(s) for visiting
  supporters

1 Buckingham Road
2 Oliver Road
3 A112 High Road Leyton
4 To Leyton Tube Station
  (¼ mile)
5 Brisbane Road
6 Windsor Road
7 To Leyton Midland Road
  BR station
8 South Stand
9 West Stand
10 Main (East) Stand
11 North Stand

↟ North direction (approx)

◄ 701334
▼ 701336

C Club Offices
S Club Shop

1 Family Stand
2 Sincil Bank
3 Sausthorpe Street
4 Cross Street
5 Co-op Community Stand
(away)
6 A158 South Park Avenue
7 Stacey West Stand
8 Lincoln Central BR Station
(½ mile)

↑ North direction (approx)

◄ 700580
▼ 700587

lincoln city
Sincil Bank, Lincoln LN5 8LD

website: **WWW.REDIMPS.COM**
e:mail: **LCFC@REDIMPS.COM**
tel no: **0870 899 2005**
colours: **RED AND WHITE STRIPES, BLACK SHORTS**
nickname: **THE IMPS**
season 2008/09: **LEAGUE TWO**

Under John Schofield the Imps, who in previous seasons had been almost permanent fixtures in the Play-Offs, started the season poorly and, following Schofield's departure, at the end of October, the experienced ex-Huddersfield boss Peter Jackson was appointed the new manager at Sincil Bank. Although the club's League form initially remained poor, the team did achieve a notable 1-1 draw at home against high-flying League One outfit Nottingham Forest in the first round of the FA Cup. There was, however, to be one highly emotional match: for the first time since 1985 and the Valley Parade fire, Lincoln City played a League match at Bradford City. The occasion was all the more poignant as Peter Jackson had been Bradford's captain on that ill-fated occasion. Under Jackson, the club's League form gradually improved and the team moved slowly up the table. Whilst not capable of reaching the Play-Offs for the umpteenth time, finishing ultimately in 15th place was considerably better than looked likely at one stage and offers a reasonable starting point for the new season. Jackson is an experienced manager and should be able to make the Imps again a force capable of reaching the Play-Offs at least.

Tel No: 0870 899 2005
Advance Tickets Tel No: 0870 899 2005
Fax: 01522 880020
Training Ground: The Sports Ground, Carlton Boulevard, Lincoln LN2 4WJ
Brief History: Founded 1884. Former Ground: John O'Gaunts Ground, moved to Sincil Bank in 1895. Founder-members 2nd Division Football League (1892). Relegated from 4th Division in 1987, promoted from GM Vauxhall Conference in 1988. Record attendance 23,196
(Total) Current Capacity: 10,130 (all seated)
Visiting Supporters' Allocation: 2,000 in Co-op Community Stand (part, remainder for Home fans)
Nearest Railway Station: Lincoln Central
Parking (Car): City centre car parks; limited on-street parking
Parking (Coach/Bus): South Common
Police Force and Tel No: Lincolnshire (01522 529911)
Disabled Visitors' Facilities:
Wheelchairs: The Simons and South (Mundy) Park stands
Blind: No special facility
Anticipated Development(s): Following the replacement of the seats in the Stacey West Stand, Sincil Bank is once again an all-seater stadium.

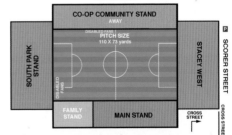

SINCIL BANK

CO-OP COMMUNITY STAND
AWAY

SOUTH PARK STAND

DISABLED FANS
PITCH SIZE
110 X 73 yards

STACEY WEST

SCORER STREET

DISABLED FANS

FAMILY STAND

MAIN STAND

CROSS STREET

CROSS STREET

liverpool

Anfield, Anfield Road, Liverpool L4 0TH

website: **WWW.LIVERPOOLFC.TV**
tel no: **0151 263 2361**
colours: **RED SHIRTS, RED SHORTS**
nickname: **THE REDS**
season 2008/09: **FA PREMIERSHIP**

season 07/08: Premier League **4TH** p**38** w**21** d**13** l**4** gf**67** ga**28**

Ultimately a highly frustrating season for Liverpool fans as strife off the field — largely as a result of the American co-owners falling out amongst themselves over the refinancing of the debt they incurred in buying the club and with the Dubai Investment Co hovering in the background — undoubtedly had an impact upon form on the field. In terms of the Premier League, Liverpool again finished fourth — thereby ensuring entry into the Champions League — although the club was pushed hard by Everton until the final stages of the season. In the FA Cup Liverpool were almost embarrassed at Anfield by non-league Havant & Waterlooville — although ultimately winning — before being humbled at home by Championship outfit Barnsley in the 5th round. For much of the campaign it looked as though Liverpool's best chance of silverware was again via the Champions League, but this too disappeared when, for the first time at this stage of the competition, Rafa Benitez's team lost out to Chelsea. As far as 2008/09 is concerned, the League again looks beyond the team and any success may well be through the cup competitions. However, with uncertainty in the board room and with Benitez apparently having to sell before being able to recruit, the dissatisfaction shown by some of the club's high profile players means that all is not rosy for the red half of Merseyside.

Advance Tickets Tel No: 0870 220 2345
Fax: 0151 260 8813
Ticket Enquiries Fax: 0151 261 1416
Training Ground: Melwood Drive, West Derby, Liverpool L12 8SV; Tel: 0151 282 8888
Brief History: Founded 1892. Anfield Ground formerly Everton F.C. Ground. Joined Football League in 1893. Record attendance 61,905
(Total) Current Capacity: 45,362 (all seated)
Visiting Supporters' Allocation: 1,972 (all seated) in Anfield Road Stand
Nearest Railway Station: Kirkdale
Parking (Car): Stanley car park
Parking (Coach/Bus): Priory Road and Pinehurst Avenue
Police Force and Tel No: Merseyside (0151 709 6010)
Disabled Visitors' Facilities:
Wheelchairs: Kop and Main Stands
Blind: Commentary available
Anticipated Development(s): The plans for the club's relocation received a boost in September 2006 when the council agreed to grant the club a 999-year lease on part of Stanley Park. The new ground, to be located some 300yd from Anfield, was scheduled to be completed for the start of the 2010/11 season and will cost some £210 million for a ground with a 60,000-seat capacity. Later in September it was announced that European funding for the associated redevelopment scheme of the Stanley Park area — a requirement of the planning permission — had also been secured; this funding allows the club to access funds from the council and the Development Agency again to part fund this work. During the 2006/07 season, the club was acquired by two Americans; as part of their post-takeover review, the two looked at the possibility of expanding the size of the new ground. Whilst work on developing the new ground progresses, the boardroom split between the US owners and the future ownership of the club may lead to some revision of the final scheme.

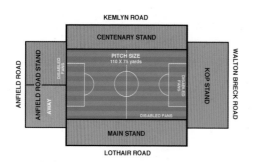

C Club Offices
S Club Shop

1 Car Park
2 Anfield Road
3 A5089 Walton Breck Road
4 Kemlyn Road
5 Kirkdale BR Station
  (1 mile)
6 Utting Avenue
7 Stanley Park
8 Spion Kop
9 Anfield Road Stand

⬆ *North direction (approx)*

◀ 700015
▼ 700030

C Club Offices
E Entrance(s) for visiting supporters
R Refreshment bars for visiting supporters
T Toilets for visiting supporters

1 To M1 Junction 11
2 Wimborne Road
3 Kenilworth Road
4 Oak Road
5 Dunstable Road
6 Luton BR Station (1 mile)
7 Ticket Office

↑ *North direction (approx)*

▸ 699805
▾ 699816

luton town

Kenilworth Road Stadium, 1 Maple Road, Luton, LU4 8AW

website: **WWW.LUTONTOWN.PREMIUMTV.CO.UK**
e:mail: **CLUBSEC@LUTONTOWN.CO.UK**
tel no: **01582 411622**
colours: **WHITE SHIRTS, BLACK SHORTS**
nickname: **THE HATTERS**
season 2008/09: **LEAGUE TWO**

A traumatic season for Luton Town saw certain of the club's officials charged by the FA with financial irregularities, the club enter Administration (with the consequent docking of 10 points), a large number of players depart as a result during the January transfer window and, following his announcement that he and his coaches would depart in early February, the termination of manager Kevin Blackwell's contract in mid-January. Blackwell was replaced on a caretaker basis by Mick Harford. It was an impossible task for Harford to keep the Hatters in League One and, even without the 10-point deduction, the club's relegation was confirmed before the end of the season. Away from the League, there was one high point in an otherwise depressing season — a 3-1 home victory over Charlton Athletic in the 3rd round of the Carling Cup. Relegated to League Two, Luton's fortunes in the fourth tier of English football will depend upon the club's ability to attract players given the circumstances. Teams relegated with Administration looming over them have historically struggled to perform at the lower level and it's probable that Luton will do the same; moreover, although the club has now exited Administration, it has been hit by a new penalty that will mean that it starts the 2008/09 season on an unprecedented minus 30 points. A season of consolidation at the new lower level is perhaps the best that the club can look forward to with relegation, given the point deduction, a very serious probability.

Advance Tickets Tel No: 01582 416976
Fax: 01582 405070
Training Ground: Ely Way, Luton LU4 9GN
Brief History: Founded 1885 from an amalgamation of Wanderers F.C. and Excelsior F.C. Former Grounds: Dallow Lane & Dunstable Road, moved to Kenilworth Road in 1905. Record attendance 30,069
(Total) Current Capacity: 10,300 (all seated)
Visiting Supporters' Allocation: 2,200
Nearest Railway Station: Luton
Parking (Car): Street parking
Parking (Coach/Bus): Luton bus station
Police Force and Tel No: Bedfordshire (01582 401212)
Disabled Visitors' Facilities:
Wheelchairs: Kenilworth Road and Main stands
Blind: Commentary available
Anticipated Development(s): One of a number of clubs to enter Administration following the collapse of ITV Digital, in the summer of 2004 it was announced that the new consortium hoping to take-over the club still intended to relocate, but there is still no definite timescale. A new owner, David Pinkney, was confirmed during July 2007; he reaffirmed the intention that the club was still planning to relocate to a new 25,000-seat stadium although there was no confirmed time-frame. The whole position is again in doubt following the club's second period of Administration and relegation to League Two.

*relegated; 10 points deducted for going into Administration

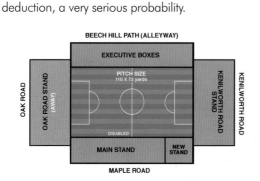

macclesfield town

Moss Rose Ground, London Road, Macclesfield, SK11 7SP

website: **WWW.MTFC.PREMIUMTV.CO.UK**
e:mail: **OFFICE@MTFC.CO.UK**
tel no: **01625 264686**
colours: **ROYAL BLUE SHIRTS, ROYAL BLUE SHORTS**
nickname: **THE SILKMEN**
season 2008/09: **LEAGUE TWO**

Towards the end of February, with the Silkmen just above the drop zone, but having played more games than the two teams below them, Keith Alexander was brought in as new manager. Previous boss Ian Brightwell was offered the chance to become Alexander's number two but declined and thus left the club. Under Alexander the club was ultimately to finish in 19th position some eight points above relegated Mansfield Town but, with both Wrexham and Mansfield picking up points towards the end of the season, Macclesfield's survival was by no means guaranteed. Away from the League, the club also suffered the embarrassment of a 3-1 away defeat at non-league Rushden & Diamonds in the 2nd round of the FA Cup. For 2008/09, it's hard to escape the conclusion that Macclesfield will again be one of the clubs more concerned with avoiding the drop rather than the promotion hunt.

Advance Tickets Tel No: 01625 264686
Fax: 01625 264692
Training Ground: Details omitted at club's request
Brief History: Founded 1874. Previous ground: Rostron Field moved to Moss Rose Ground in 1891. Winners of the Vauxhall Conference in 1994/95 and 1997/97. Admitted to Football League for 1997/98 season. Record attendance 10,041
(Total) Current Capacity: 6,335 (2,599 seated)
Visiting Supporters' Allocation: 1,900 (1,500 in Silkman Terrace; 400 seated in Estate Road Stand)
Nearest Railway Station: Macclesfield
Parking (Car): No parking at the ground and the nearest off-street car park is in the town centre (25min walk). There is some on-street parking in the vicinity, but this can get crowded.
Parking (Coach/Bus): As directed
Police Force and Tel No: Cheshire (01625 610000)
Disabled Visitors' Facilities:
Wheelchairs: 45 places in Estate Road Stand
Blind: No special facility
Anticipated Development(s): The club is examining the possibility of relocating to a new 10,000-capacity stadium as part of the Dane's Moss redevelopment.

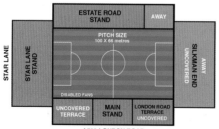

C Club Offices
E Entrance(s) for visiting
  supporters

1 A523 London Road
2 To Town Centre and BR
  station (1.5 miles)
3 To Leek
4 Moss Lane
5 Star Lane
6 Site of Silkmans Public House
  (now demolished)
7 Star Lane End
8 Silkman End (away section)
9 Estate Road Stand

↑ *North direction (approx)*

◄ 700602
▼ 700598

1 A662 Ashton New Road
2 Commonwealth Boulevard
3 Stadium Way
4 A6010 Alan Turing Way
5 North Stand
6 South (Key 103) Stand
7 West (Colin Bell) Stand
8 East Stand
9 National Squash Centre
10 Warm-up track
11 To Manchester city centre and
   Piccadilly station
   (1½ miles)

⬆ North direction (approx)

▸ 700078
▾ 700072

manchester city

The City of Manchester Stadium, Sportcity, Manchester M11 3FF

website: **WWW.MCFC.CO.UK**
e:mail: **MCFC@MCFC.CO.UK**
tel no: **0870 062 1894**
colours: **SKY BLUE SHIRTS, WHITE SHORTS**
nickname: **THE BLUES**
season 2008/09: **PREMIER LEAGUE**

A season of considerable promise at the start, with a new owner in ex-Thailand Prime Minister Thaksin Shinawatra and new manager in the guise of ex-England supremo Sven Goran Eriksson, seemed to be on the point of fulfilment as the early results showed a considerable improvement over those of 2006/07. The club's home form, in particular, ensured that there was little danger of the team being dragged into the relegation battle and, in finishing ninth, Eriksson delivered his promise of a top ten finish. However, if the season started with high hopes, it ended in high farce with uncertainty over the future of the manager — with the owner rumoured to be dissatisfied with the ultimate position and doubts over some of Eriksson's recruits — and in an embarrassing 8-1 defeat in the final League game of the season away at Middlesbrough. City were another Premier League team to struggle against lower league opposition, falling to a 2-1 home defeat by Sheffield United in the 4th round of the FA Cup. During the close season in 2007, City were at a disadvantage in the transfer market as a result of the tortuous purchase of the club by Thaksin and the later appointment of Eriksson; given the current trials and tribulations, it's hard to escape the conclusion that history may repeat itself in 2008 with new manager Mark Hughes faced by a relatively short time frame before the closure of the transfer window. City, provided that the club can retain its star players in the face of disquiet over the handling of Eriksson and can recruit sensibly in the close season, should again have the potential for a top-half finish but anything beyond that looks unrealistic.

Advance Tickets Tel No: 0870 062 1894
Fax: 0161 438 7999
Training Ground: Platt Lane Complex, Yew Tree Road, Fallowfield, Manchester M14 7UU; Tel: 0161 248 6610; Fax: 0161 257 0030
Brief History: Founded 1880 at West Gorton, changed name to Ardwick (reformed 1887) and to Manchester City in 1894. Former grounds: Clowes Street (1880-81), Kirkmanshulme Cricket Club (1881-82), Queens Road (1882-84), Pink Bank Lane (1884-87), Hyde Road (1887-1923) and Maine Road (from 1923 until 2003). Moved to the City of Manchester Stadium for the start of the 2003/04 season. Founder-members 2nd Division (1892). Record attendance (at Maine Road) 84,569 (record for a Football League Ground); at City of Manchester Stadium 47,321
(Total) Current Capacity: 48,000 (All seated)
Visiting Supporters' Allocation: 3,000 (South Stand); can be increased to 4,500 if required
Nearest Railway Station: Manchester Piccadilly
Parking (Car): Ample match day parking available to the north of the stadium, entrance via Alan Turing Way. On-street parking restrictions operate in all areas adjacent to the stadium on matchdays.
Parking (Coach/Bus): Coach parking for visiting supporters is adjacent to turnstiles at Key 103 Stand. For home supporters to the north of the stadium, entrance from Alan Turing Way.
Police Force and Tel No: Greater Manchester (0161 872 5050)
Disabled Visitors' facilities:
Wheelchairs: 300 disabled seats around ground
Blind: 14 places alongside helpers in East Stand Level 1. Commentary available via headsets.

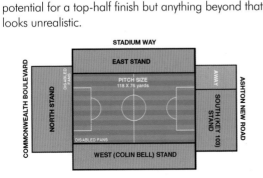

manchester united

Old Trafford, Sir Matt Busby Way, Manchester, M16 0RA

website: **WWW.MANUTD.COM**
e:mail: **ENQUIRIES@MANUTD.CO.UK**
tel no: **0161 868 8000**
colours: **RED SHIRTS, WHITE SHORTS**
nickname: **THE RED DEVILS**
season 2008/09: **PREMIER LEAGUE**

season 07/08: Premier League **1ST** *p***38** *w***27** *d***5** *l***5** *gf***83** *ga***27**

A season that was overshadowed to a certain extent by the fact that it marked the 50th anniversary of the Munich Disaster — an event commemorated impeccably in an emotional Manchester Derby — was ultimately to prove one of the most successful in United's history as the club won both the Premier League title and, for the third time, the Champions League. Initially, it was Arsenal that seemed to have the edge in the former, but the Gunners seemed to suffer an irreversible decline in form, allowing Sir Alex Ferguson's team to seize the advantage but Chelsea under Avram Grant were to prove more serious challengers for the League title, particularly after their victory over United at Stamford Bridge. For the first time in a number of years, the final destination of the title was not resolved until the last day of the season with both United and Chelsea equal on points but with the former having a superior goal difference. In the event United's victory at Wigan was more than sufficient as Chelsea could only draw at home against Bolton. It was also Chelsea that offered United its opposition in the final of the Champions League, as history was made when, for the first time, two English clubs competed for the trophy. In a pulsating final held in Moscow, United were ultimately to triumph on penalties after the match had ended 1-1 after extra time. For 2008/09 who would bet against United again securing the League title and being serious contenders in the various cup competitions. Now in his late 60s, there seems to be little diminution in Ferguson's desire to win trophies and the club will undoubtedly be a force again next campaign.

Advance Tickets Tel No: 0870 442 1999

Fax: 0161 868 8804

Training Ground: Carrington Training Complex, Birch Road, Manchester M31 4HH

Brief History: Founded in 1878 as 'Newton Heath L&Y', later Newton Heath, changed to Manchester United in 1902. Former Grounds: North Road, Monsall & Bank Street, Clayton, moved to Old Trafford in 1910 (used Manchester City F.C. Ground 1941-49). Founder-members Second Division (1892).
Record attendance 76,962

(Total) Current Capacity: 76,100 (All seated)

Visiting Supporters' Allocation: Approx. 3,000 in corner of South and East Stands

Nearest Railway Station: At Ground

Parking (Car): Lancashire Cricket Ground and White City

Parking (Coach/Bus): As directed by Police

Police Force and Tel No: Greater Manchester (0161 872 5050)

Disabled Visitors' Facilities:
Wheelchairs: South East Stand
Blind: Commentary available

Anticipated Development(s): The work on the £45 million project construct infills at the north-east and north-west corners of the ground has now been completed and takes Old Trafford's capacity to 76,000, making it by some margin the largest league ground in Britain. Any future development of the ground will involve the Main (South) stand although work here is complicated by the proximity of the building to the adjacent railway line.

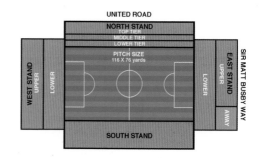

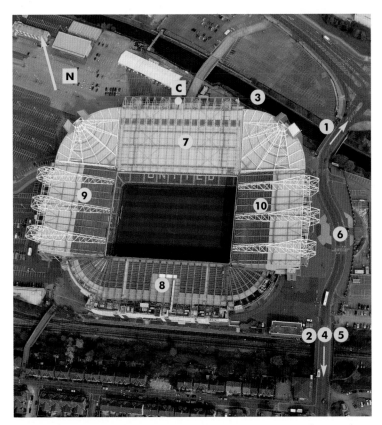

C Club Offices

1 To A5081 Trafford Park Road
  to M63 Junction 4 (5 miles)
2 A56 Chester Road
3 Bridgewater Canal
4 To Old Trafford Cricket
  Ground
5 To Parking and Warwick Road
  BR Station
6 Sir Matt Busby Way
7 North Stand
8 South Stand
9 West Stand
10 East Stand

↑ North direction (approx)

◂ 701060
▾ 701063

▲ 700627
▶ 700621

C Club Offices
S Club Shop
1 Cargo Fleet Road
2 To Middlesbrough
   railway station
3 To Middlesbrough
   town centre
4 Middlesbrough Docks
5 Shepherdson Way to A66
6 South Stand
7 Car parks

⬆ *North direction (approx)*

middlesbrough

Riverside Stadium, Middlesbrough, Cleveland TS3 6RS

website: **WWW.MFC.CO.UK**
e:mail: **ENQUIRIES@MFC.CO.UK**
tel no: **0844 499 6789**
colours: **RED SHIRTS, RED SHORTS**
nickname: **BORO**
season 2008/09: **PREMIER LEAGUE**

A difficult season for the Riverside faithful saw Gareth Southgate's team hovering just above the drop zone for much of the campaign; although never seriously threatened, if results, had, however, gone slightly differently then, undoubtedly, Boro' could have been sucked into the mire and it was only on the penultimate weekend of the season, when Portsmouth were defeated 2-0, that mathematically the team was safe for another season. Ironically, given the infrequency with which Boro' found the back of the net — only 35 times in 37 matches leading up to the final game of the season — one of the most remarkable results of the season occurred on the final Sunday when Boro' trounced Manchester City 8-1. Provided that Southgate can attract a proven goalscorer to the Riverside, Boro' should again ensure Premier League survival in 2008/09 but perhaps a position of mid-table mediocrity is the best that can be hoped for.

Advance Tickets Tel No: 0844 499 1234
Fax: 01642 757690
Training Ground: Rockcliffe Park, Hurworth Place, Near Darlington, County Durham DL2 2DU; Tel: 01325 722222
Brief History: Founded 1876. Former Grounds: Archery Ground (Albert Park), Breckon Hill Road, Linthorpe Road, moved to Ayresome Park in 1903, and to current ground in Summer 1995. F.A. Amateur Cup winners 1894 and 1897 (joined Football League in 1899). Record attendance (Ayresome Park) 53,596, (Riverside Stadium) 35,000
(Total) Current Capacity: 35,100 (All seated)
Visiting Supporters' Allocation: 3,450 (in the South Stand)
Nearest Railway Station: Middlesbrough
Parking (Car): All parking at stadium is for permit holders Parking (Coach/Bus): As directed
Police Force and Tel No: Cleveland (01642 248184)
Disabled Visitors' Facilities:
Wheelchairs: More than 170 places available for disabled fans; *Blind*: Commentary available
Anticipated Development(s): There remain long term plans for the ground's capacity to be increased to 42,000 through the construction of extra tiers on the North, South and East stands, although there is no confirmed timetable for this work at the current time.

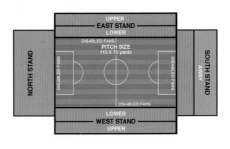

millwall

New Den, Bolina Road, London, SE16 3LN

website: **WWW.MILLWALLFC.PREMIUMTV.CO.UK**
e:mail: **QUESTION@MILLWALLPLC.COM**
tel no: **020 7232 1222**
colours: **BLUE SHIRTS, WHITE SHORTS**
nickname: **THE LIONS**
season 2008/09: **LEAGUE ONE**

season 07/08: League One **17TH** p**46** w**14** d**10** l**22** gf**45** ga**60**

Following Willie Donachie's appointment during the course of the 2006/07 season, the club's form picked up sufficiently to lift the Lions towards the Play-Off places and hopes were high in 2007/08 that the club would sustain this performance and make a more sustained push towards reclaiming a place in the Championship. These hopes were, however, to be dashed and the team found itself drifting towards the wrong end of the table. In early November, Kenny Jackett was appointed the new manager and under him the threat of relegation to League Two was averted, although it was a close run thing. Ultimately the team finished in 17th place, some four points above relegated Bournemouth but a considerable distance below the position achieved in 2006/07. For the new season, the Lions ought to be capable of making a more serious push towards the top half of the table but a position of mid-table mediocrity looks the most likely result come May 2009.

Advance Tickets Tel No: 020 7231 9999
Fax: 020 7231 3663
Training Ground: Millwall FC Training Ground, Calmont Road (off Ashgrove Road), Bromley Hill, Bromley, Kent BR1 4BZ

Brief History: Founded 1885 as Millwall Rovers, changed name to Millwall Athletic (1889) and Millwall (1925). Former Grounds: Glengall Road, East Ferry Road (two separate grounds), North Greenwich Ground and The Den – Cold Blow Lane – moved to New Den 1993/94 season. Founder-members Third Division (1920). Record attendance (at The Den) 48,672 (at New Den) 20,093

(Total) Current Capacity: 20,150 (All seated)

Visiting Supporters' Allocation: 4,382 in North Stand

Nearest Railway Station: South Bermondsey or Surrey Docks (Tube)

Parking (Car): Juno Way car parking (8 mins walk)

Parking (Coach/Bus): At Ground

Police Force and Tel No: Metropolitan (0207 679 9217)

Disabled Visitors' Facilities:
Wheelchairs: 200 spaces in West Stand Lower Tier
Blind: Commentary available

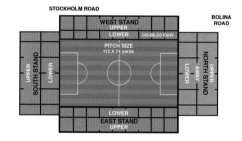

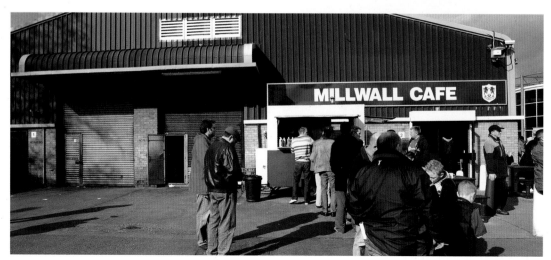

C Club Offices
S Club Shop
E Entrance(s) for visiting
  supporters

1 Bolina Road
2 South Bermondsey station
3 Footpath to station for away
  fans
4 Zampa Road
5 Stockholm Road
6 North Stand (away)

↑ North direction (approx)

◀ 697379
▼ 697384

1 B4034 Saxon Street
2 A5
3 Grafton Street
4 Bletcham Way
5 Away Area
6 A5 Southbound to London
7 A5 Northbound to Milton
  Keynes centre and Towcester
8 To Bletchley railway station
  (two miles)
9 To Milton Keynes Central
  railway station (four miles)

↑ North direction (approx)

▸ 701140
▾ 701148

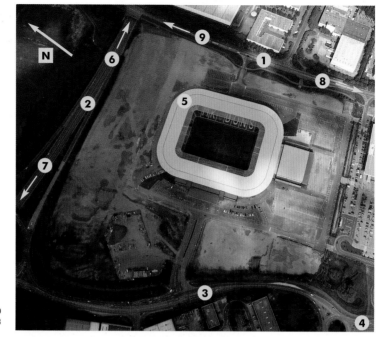

milton keynes dons

Stadium:mk, Stadium Way West, Milton Keynes, MK1 1ST

website: **WWW.MKDONS.PREMIUMTV.CO.UK**
e:mail: **INFO@MKDONS.CO.UK**
tel no: **01908 622922**
colours: **WHITE SHIRTS, WHITE SHORTS**
nickname: **THE DONS**
season 2008/09: **LEAGUE ONE**

A season of considerable success both on and off the pitch saw Milton Keynes Dons move into the club's brand-new stadium and, having been in the promotion places for the bulk of the season, achieve the League Two title prior to the final Saturday of the season. During the course of the season the club, which had lost out in the Play-Offs in 2006/07, proved too strong for many and, conceding only 37 League goals during the entire campaign, had the strongest defence in League Two with only Nottingham Forest improving on that total throughout the Football League. With Paul Ince now departed to take over as manager at Blackburn Rovers, new manager Roberto di Matteo will face the challenge – by no means impossible – of keeping the Dons at this higher level.

Advance Tickets Tel No: 01908 622900
Fax: 01908 622933
Training Ground: Woughton on the Green, Milton Keynes
Brief History: Founded 1889 as Wimbledon Old Centrals, changed name to Wimbledon in 1905 and to Milton Keynes Dons in 2004. Former grounds: Wimbledon Common, Pepy's Road, Grand Drive, Merton Hall Road, Malden Wanderers Cricket Ground, Plough Lane, Selhurst Park (1991-2002) and National Hockey Stadium (2002-2007); moved to Stadium:MK for start of the 2007/08 season. Elected to the Football League in 1997. Record attendance (Plough Lane) 18,000; (Selhurst Park) 30,115; (National Hockey Stadium) 5,306; (Stadium:MK) 20,222
(Total) Current Capacity: 22,000 (All seated)
Visiting Supporters' Allocation: c3000 in North East Corner
Nearest Railway Station: Bletchley (two miles); Milton Keynes Central (four miles)
Parking (Car): The ground is located with a retail development and parking restrictions at the ground will probably apply
Parking (Coach/Bus): As directed
Police Force and Tel No: Thames Valley Police (01865 846000)
Disabled Visitors' Facilities:
Wheelchairs: 164 spaces;
Blind: new facility for 2008/09 season
Anticipated Development(s): Following a number of years at the National Hockey Stadium, the Milton Keynes Dons moved into the new Stadium: MK for the start of the 2007/08 season. The ground has been designed to facilitate the addition of a second tier of seating if required in the future, taking the total capacity to 30,000.

season 07/08: League Two **1ST** (promoted) p**46** w**29** d**10** l**7** gf**82** ga**37**

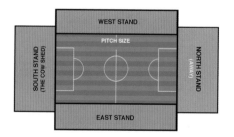

117

morecambe

Christie Park, Lancaster Road, Morecambe, Lancashire, LA4 5TJ

website: **WWW.MORCAMBEFC.COM**
e:mail: **OFFICE@MORCAMBEFC.COM**
tel no: **01524 411797**
colours: **RED SHIRTS, WHITE SHORTS**
nickname: **SHRIMPS**
season 2008/09: **LEAGUE TWO**

Promoted at the end of the 2006/07 season from the Conference, Sammy McIlroy's side prospered in the Football League and, whilst never seriously threatening to break into the battle for the Play-Off places, finishing 11th in the club's first season in the League was a highly creditable performance. It was not only in the League that the club surprised many; in the Carling Cup the team had impressive victories away from home in the competition over Championship opposition. In the first round victory over Preston North End was achieved at Deepdale 2-1 whilst, in the second round, Wolves were defeated 3-1 after extra time. For the new season, there is always the threat of 'second seasonitis' but McIlroy is an astute manager and the club should be able to consolidate further its League status whilst an outside chance of the Play-Offs shouldn't be discounted.

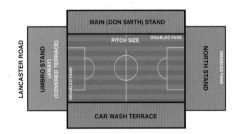

Advance Tickets Tel No: 01524 411797
Fax: 01524 832230
Training Ground: New facility being sought for the 2008/09 season
Brief History: Founded 1920. Previous grounds: Morecambe Cricket Ground; moved to Roseberry Park 1921; ground later renamed Christie Park after the club's president who had funded its purchase. Joined Conference at the end of the 1995/96 season and promoted to the Football league at the end of the 2006/07 season. Record attendance 9,234
(Total) Current Capacity: 6,400 (1,200 seated)
Visiting Supporters' Allocation: 1,500 (Umbro Stand — all standing) plus limited number of seats in Main Stand
Nearest Railway Station: Morecambe
Parking (Car): Main car park is pass only; there is a second small car park otherwise on-street only
Parking (Coach/Bus): As directed
Other clubs sharing ground: Blackburn Rovers Reserves
Police Force and Tel No: Lancashire Constabulary (0845 125 3545)
Disabled Visitors' Facilities:
Wheelchairs: 36 home and 10 away spaces
Blind: No special facility
Anticipated Development(s): Having previously announced plans to redevelop Christie Park, the club has now decided to relocate to a new 6,000-seater stadium. If all goes according o plan, the new stadium could be available for the start of the 2010/11 season.

1 B5321 Lancaster Road
2 Lathom Avenue
3 Christie Avenue
4 To Morecambe town centre
and railway station (one mile)
5 To A589
6 Ennerdale Avenue
7 Roseberry Avenue
8 Burlington Avenue
9 North Stand
10 Main Stand
11 Umbro Stand (away)
12 Car Wash Terrace

↑ North direction (approx)

◄ 700865
▼ 700870

C Club Offices
S Club Shop

1 St. James's Park
2 Strawberry Place
3 Gallowgate
4 Away Section
5 To Newcastle Central BR
Station (1/2 mile) &
A6127(M)
6 Car Park
7 Barrack Road (A189)
8 To A1 and North
9 Corporation Street
10 Gallowgate End
11 Metro Station
12 Sir John Hall Stand
13 Millburn Stand
14 East Stand

⬆ *North direction (approx)*

▸ 700356
▾ 700351

newcastle united
St James's Park, Newcastle-upon-Tyne, NE1 4ST

website: **WWW.NUFC.PREMIUMTV.CO.UK**
e:mail: **CONTACT VIA WEBSITE**
tel no: **0191 201 8400**
colours: **BLACK AND WHITE STRIPED SHIRTS, WHITE SHORTS**
nickname: **THE MAGPIES**
season 2008/09: **PREMIER LEAGUE**

The poisoned chalice that is the managerial position at St James's Park claimed another high profile victim when Sam Allardyce was sacked following a series of poor League results and a 0-0 draw away at Stoke City in the Third Round of the FA Cup. Allardyce, appointed only eight months earlier, had overseen the Magpies in some 24 matches but his position was weakened by the sale of the club, shortly after his appointment, to Mike Ashley. Nigel Pearson was appointed caretaker and his unenviable first task was to prepare a team for the daunting trip to Old Trafford and an in-form Manchester United. A 6-0 trouncing showed the extent of the job for new manager Kevin Keegan, who returned to the club for a second spell in charge just in time to see his new team defeat Stoke City 4-1 in the FA Cup Third Round replay. Initially it looked as though the arrival of 'King Kev' was going to do little to arrest what seemed to be an irresistible decline towards the drop zone as games were lost and goals conceded in large numbers. However, as the season drew to a close, the team's confidence and form were restored and, aided by Michael Owen rediscovering his scoring ability, a number of decent results were achieved, ensuring a position of mid-table mediocrity at the end. At the end of the season, Keegan expressed his concern that it was now virtually impossible to see how a team like Newcastle could break the stranglehold on the Premier League exerted by the 'Big Four'; whilst the sentiments are undoubtedly accurate, it's a statement that owner Mike Ashley and the Toon faithful will find concerning. With Keegan at the helm, United should easily achieve a top-half finish but it's hard to disagree with Keegan that the best that can be hoped for is fifth position.

Advance Tickets Tel No: 0191 261 1571
Fax: 0191 201 8600
Training Ground: Darsley Park, Whitley Road, Benton, Newcastle upon Tyne NE12 9FA
Brief History: Founded in 1882 as Newcastle East End, changed to Newcastle United in 1892. Former Grounds: Chillingham Road, moved to St. James' Park (former home of defunct Newcastle West End) in 1892. Record attendance 68,386
(Total) Current Capacity: 52,316 (all seated)
Visiting Supporters' Allocation: 3,000 in North West Stand
Nearest Railway Station: Newcastle Central
Parking (Car): Leazes car park and street parking
Parking (Coach/Bus): Leazes car park
Police Force and Tel No: Northumbria (0191 232 3451)
Disabled Visitors' Facilities:
Wheelchairs: 103 spaces available
Blind: Commentary available
Anticipated Development(s): The club announced plans in March 2007 for a £300 million scheme to increase capacity at St James's Park to 60,000. The work, which would include the construction of a hotel and conference city, will see the expansion of the Gallowgate End. The project, which has yet to receive planning consent, has no confirmed timescale at present.

season 07/08: PremierLeague 12TH p38 w11 d10 l17 gf45 ga65

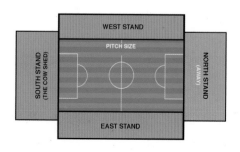

WEST STAND
PITCH SIZE
SOUTH STAND (THE COW SHED)
NORTH STAND (AWAY)
EAST STAND

northampton town

Sixfields Stadium, Northampton NN5 5QA

website: **WWW.NTFC.PREMIUMTV.CO.UK**
e:mail: **PAULA.KANE@NTFC.TV**
tel no: **01604 683700**
colours: **CLARET WITH WHITE SLEEVED SHIRTS, WHITE SHORTS**
nickname: **THE COBBLERS**
season 2008/09: **LEAGUE ONE**

One of the teams in the pack chasing the Play-Offs, Stuart Gray's Northampton Town were ultimately to finish in ninth place some 10 points adrift of Southend United in sixth place. As with other teams in the top half of the League One outside the top six, the Cobblers looked capable of achieving a Play-Off place for periods of the season but lacked the consistency to prolong a sustained promotion push. However, provided that the progress achieved in 2007/08 can be maintained into the new season, the team should again feature as one of those aspiring for a Play-Off place.

Advance Tickets Tel No: 01604 683777
Fax: 01604 751613
Training Ground: No specific facility
Brief History: Founded 1897. Former, County, Ground was part of Northamptonshire County Cricket Ground. Moved to Sixfields Stadium during early 1994/95 season. Record attendance 24,523 (at County Ground); 7,557 (at Sixfields)
(Total) Current Capacity: 7,653 (All seated)
Visiting Supporters' Allocation: 850 (in Paul Cox Panel and Paint South Stand; can be increased to 1,150 if necessary)
Nearest Railway Station: Northampton
Parking (Car): Adjacent to Ground
Parking (Coach/Bus): Adjacent to Ground
Police Force and Tel No: Northants (01604 700700)
Disabled Visitors' Facilities:
Wheelchairs: Available on all four sides
Blind: Available
Anticipated Development(s): The club has plans to increase the capacity of the Sixfields stadium to c16,000 all-seated although there is no timescale for this work.

C Club Offices
S Club Shop
E Entrance(s) for visiting supporters
R Refreshment bars for visiting supporters
T Toilets for visiting supporters

1 South Stand (away)
2 Athletics Stand
3 Upton Way
4 Car parks
5 A45 towards A43 (Towcester and A5)
6 To Weedon Road
7 To Town Centre and station
8 A45 to M1 (Jct 16)

↑ *North direction (approx)*

◀ 699879
▼ 699819

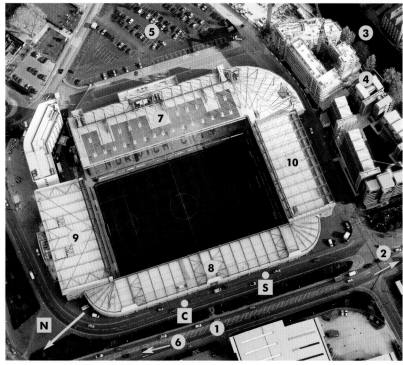

▲ 700801
▶ 700795

C Club Offices
S Club Shop

1 Carrow Road
2 A47 King Street
3 River Wensum
4 Riverside
5 Car Park
6 To Norwich BR Station
7 South (Jarrold) Stand
8 Geoffrey Watling (City) Stand
9 Barclay End Stand
10 The Norwich & Peterborough
(River End) Stand

↑ North direction (approx)

norwich city

Carrow Road , Norwich, NR1 1JE

website: **WWW.CANARIES.PREMIUMTV.CO.UK**
e:mail: **RECEPTION@NCFC-CANARIES.CO.UK**
tel no: **01603 760760**
colours: **YELLOW SHIRTS, GREEN SHORTS**
nickname: **THE CANARIES**
season 2008/09: **CHAMPIONSHIP**

In early October, following the club's 1-0 defeat at QPR — Rangers' first win of the League campaign — a result that left City in the League Championship drop zone, Peter Grant left the Canaries by mutual consent. He was replaced as caretaker manager by Jim Duffy. At the end of October, the Canaries appointed ex-Newcastle boss Glenn Roeder to the Carrow Road hot-seat, although initially results in the League saw the team drop to the foot of the division form subsequently picked up. For the rest of the season, the club produced some reasonable results interspersed with a number of poor performances culminating in the 4-1 defeat at relegation threatened Sheffield Wednesday on the last day of the season. Although the Canaries finished in 17th place in the Championship, this was only three points above relegated Leicester City and, in a close battle to avoid the drop, it's easy to see how tight the margins between success and failure are. As one of a number of struggling ex-Premier League clubs in the Championship, City will have problems in trying to re-establish themselves as serious contenders for promotion but should be capable of a top-half finish.

Advance Tickets Tel No: 0870 444 1902
Fax: 01603 613886
Training Ground: Colney Training Centre, Hethersett Lane, Colney, Norwich NR4 7TS
Brief History: Founded 1902. Former grounds: Newmarket Road and the Nest, Rosary Road; moved to Carrow Road in 1935. Founder-members 3rd Division (1920). Record attendance 43,984
(Total) Current Capacity: 26,034
Visiting Supporters' Allocation: 2,500 maximum in South Stand
Nearest Railway Station: Norwich
Parking (Car): City centre car parks
Parking (Coach/Bus): Lower Clarence Road
Police Force and Tel No: Norfolk (01603 768769)
Disabled Visitors' Facilities:
Wheelchairs: New facility in corner infill stand
Blind: Commentary available
Anticipated Development(s): The £3 million corner infill between the new Jarrold (South) Stand and the River End was opened in two stages in early 2005. The upper tier provides seats for 850 and the lower for 660. There is also a new disabled area located between the two tiers. This work takes Carrow Road's capacity to 26,000. As part of the plans for the Jarrold Stand, the pitch was relocated one metre away from the City Stand; this will facilitate the construction of a second tier on the City Stand in the future if required.

season 07/08: Championship **17TH** p46 w15 d10 l21 gf49 ga59

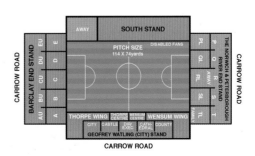

nottingham forest

City Ground, Nottingham, NG2 5FJ

website: **WWW.NOTTINGHAMFOREST.PREMIUMTV.CO.UK**
e:mail: **ENQUIRIES@NOTTINGHAMFOREST.CO.UK**
tel no: **0115 982 4444**
colours: **RED SHIRTS, WHITE SHORTS**
nickname: **THE REDS**
season 2008/09: **CHAMPIONSHIP**

season 07/08: League One **2ND** (promoted) **p46 w22 d16 l8 gf64 ga32**

After three seasons in League One, Nottingham Forest finally managed under Colin Calderwood to sustain a serious promotion challenge and, having lost out in the lottery of the Play-Offs in 2006/07, were again in a three-way battle for the second automatic promotion spot on the final Saturday. Vying with Forest to join Swansea in the League Championship were Doncaster Rovers and Carlisle United with the former occupying the all-important second place. In the final League game of the season Forest faced the previous season's Play-Off nemesis in the guise of Yeovil Town; a 3-2 home victory put the pressure on both Carlisle, who could only draw 1-1 at home against relegation-threatened Bournemouth, and Doncaster, who were ultimately defeated 2-1 at Cheltenham (a result that kept Cheltenham in League One). Thus Championship football returns to the City Ground in 2008/09 although, as other teams promoted in recent years have discovered, it will be a battle to retain this newly achieved status. Calderwood, whose failure to secure consistency in the promotion hunt during the course of the season led to some criticism, will have to work hard to keep the team up and much will depend upon how far he can build on the squad and which players move on.

Advance Tickets Tel No: 0871 226 1980
Fax: 0115 982 4455
Training Ground: Nottingham Forest Football Academy, Gresham Close, West Bridgford, Nottingham NG2 7RQ
Brief History: Founded 1865 as Forest Football Club, changed name to Nottingham Forest (c1879). Former Grounds: Forest Recreation Ground, Meadow Cricket Ground, Trent Bridge (Cricket Ground), Parkside, Gregory Ground and Town Ground, moved to City Ground in 1898. Founder-members of Second Division (1892). Record attendance 49,945
(Total) Current Capacity: 30,602 (all seated)
Visiting Supporters' Allocation: Approx 4,750
Nearest Railway Station: Nottingham
Parking (Car): East car park and street parking
Parking (Coach/Bus): East car park
Police Force and Tel No: Nottinghamshire (0115 948 1888)
Disabled Visitors' Facilities:
Wheelchairs: Front of Brian Clough Stand
Blind: No special facility
Anticipated Development(s): In late June 2007 it was announced that the club was planning a possible relocation from the City Ground to a new 50,000-seat ground at Clifton. If all goes according to plan, the club anticipates moving into the new £45-50 million ground for the start of the 2014/15 season.

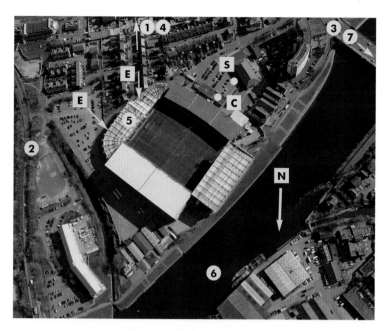

C Club Offices
S Club Shop
E Entrance(s) for visiting
  supporters

1 To Radcliffe Road
2 Lady Bay Bridge Road
3 Trent Bridge
4 To Trent Bridge Cricket
  Ground
5 Bridgford Stand
6 River Trent
7 To Nottingham Midland BR
  Station (½ mile)

 North direction (approx)

◄ 700807
▾ 700817

E Entrance(s) for visiting
supporters
R Refreshment bars for visiting
supporters
T Toilets for visiting supporters

1 A6011 Meadow Lane
2 County Road
3 A60 London Road
4 River Trent
5 Nottingham Midland BR
Station (½ mile)
6 Jimmy Sirrel Stand
7 Kop Stand (away)
8 Derek Pavis Stand
9 Family (Meadow Lane) Stand

↑ North direction (approx)

▶ 700818
▾ 700828

notts county

Meadow Lane, Nottingham, NG2 3HJ
website: **WWW.NOTTSCOUNTYFC.PREMIUMTV.CO.UK**
e:mail: **INFO@NOTTSCOUNTYFC.CO.UK**
tel no: **0115 952 9000**
colours: **BLACK AND WHITE STRIPED SHIRTS, WHITE SHORTS**
nickname: **THE MAGPIES**
season 2008/09: **LEAGUE TWO**

A season of considerable trouble for Steve Thompson's side saw County struggle to make an impact on the League and, for a long period of the season, it looked as though County — one of the oldest League clubs in the country — might be about to surrender its League status, particularly as it drifted towards the relegation zone at the same time as both Wrexham and Mansfield started to pick up points. In the event, however, safety was ensured on the penultimate Saturday of the season and thus County will face another season of League Two football in 2008/09. It was not only in the League where the club embarrassed itself; equally disappointing for fans was the 1-0 home defeat by non-league Havant & Waterlooville in the 2nd round of the FA Cup. Although the team's defence was particularly mean, conceding only 52 goals in the League, on a par with Rochdale and Stockport, teams that reached the Play-Offs, the team's fundamental weakness was up front, where the club scored a miserly 37 League goals all season — the lowest by some margin in the Football League. Unless Thompson is able to address the question of improving his strike force, it's likely that County will again struggle in 2008/09 to retain its League status.

Advance Tickets Tel No: 0115 955 7204
Fax: 0115 955 3994
Training Ground: Gedling Town FC, Riverside Ground, Stoke Lane, Stoke Bardolph, Nottingham NG14 5HX
Brief History: Founded 1862 (oldest club in Football League) as Nottingham, changed to Notts County in c1882. Former Grounds: Notts Cricket Ground (Beeston), Castle Cricket Ground, Trent Bridge Cricket Ground, moved to Meadow Lane in 1910. Founder-members Football League (1888). Record attendance 47,310.
(Total) Current Capacity: 20,300 (all seated)
Visiting Supporters' Allocation: 5,438 (seated)
Nearest Railway Station: Nottingham Midland
Parking (Car): Mainly street parking
Parking (Coach/Bus): Cattle market
Other clubs sharing ground: Nottingham RUFC
Police Force and Tel No: Nottingham (0115 948 1888)
Disabled Visitors' Facilities:
Wheelchairs: Meadow Lane/Jimmy Sirrel/Derek Pavis Stands
Blind: No special facility

season 07/08: League Two **21ST** p46 w10 d18 l18 gf55 ga53

COUNTY ROAD
JIMMY SIRREL STAND
DISABLED FANS
PITCH SIZE
117 x 76 yards
DISABLED FANS
CATTLE MARKET ROAD
KOP STAND AWAY
DISABLED FANS
FAMILY STAND
MEADOW LANE
DISABLED FANS
DEREK PAVIS STAND
P
IREMONGER ROAD

NOTTS COUNTY FOOTBALL CLUB
FOUNDED 1862

oldham athletic

Boundary Park, Oldham, OL1 2PA

website: **OLDHAMATHLETIC.PREMIUMTV.CO.UK**
e:mail: **ENQUIRIES@OLDHAMATHLETIC.CO.UK**
tel no: **0871 226 2235**
colours: **BLUE SHIRTS, BLUE SHORTS**
nickname: **THE LATICS**
season 2008/09: **LEAGUE ONE**

Having achieved a Play-Off place at the end of the 2006/07 season, expectations were high that John Sheridan's team would again feature in the battle for a top six finish. However, these hopes were to be dashed as the team failed to sustain any serious challenge for these all-important places. Finishing eighth — albeit nine points adrift of sixth place — does, however, provide a good foundation for a further promotion push in 2008/09. Away from the League there was also a considerable success in the 3rd round of the FA Cup when the Latics proved triumphant at Premier League Everton, winning 1-0 at Goodison Park. For 2008/09, Oldham should again have the potential to reach a Play-Off place although automatic promotion looks unrealistic.

Advance Tickets Tel No: 0871 226 2235

Fax: 0871 226 1715

Training Ground: Chapel Road, Hollins, Oldham OL8 4QQ

Brief History: Founded 1897 as Pine Villa, changed name to Oldham Athletic in 1899. Former Grounds: Berry's Field, Pine Mill, Athletic Ground (later named Boundary Park), Hudson Fold, moved to Boundary Park in 1906. Record attendance 47,671

(Total) Current Capacity: 13,624 (all seated)

Visiting Supporters' Allocation: 1,800 minimum, 4,600 maximum

Nearest Railway Station: Oldham Werneth

Parking (Car): Lookers Stand car park

Parking (Coach/Bus): At Ground

Other Clubs Sharing Ground:
Oldham Roughyeads RLFC

Police Force and Tel No: Greater Manchester (0161 624 0444)

Disabled Visitors' Facilities:
Wheelchairs: Rochdale Road and Seton Stands
Blind: No special facility

Anticipated Development(s): Although the club originally had plans to relocate, it was announced in February 2007 that it was going to seek Planning Permission late in 2007 for the redevelopment of Boundary Park. The proposed £80 million plan would see three sides of the ground rebuilt with the intention of obtaining a 16,000 capacity. The redevelopment would also include a hotel, fitness club and offices. It is likely that the first phase of the work will include the redevelopment of the existing Main Stand, with subsequent work including new stands on the south and west sides. In early November 2007, the club's planning application for the redevelopment of Boundary Park was rejected although a revised application was granted the following month.

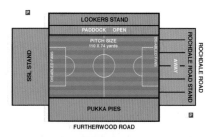

C Club Offices
E Entrance(s) for visiting
  supporters

1 A663 Broadway
2 Furtherwood Road
3 Chadderton Way
4 To A627(M) and M62
5 To Oldham Werneth BR
  Station (1½ miles)
6 Car Park
7 Rochdale Road Stand (away)
8 SSL Stand
9 Lookers Stand
10 Pukka Pies Stand

↑ North direction (approx)

◂ 700830
▾ 700840

C Club Offices
S Club Shop
E Entrance(s) for visiting supporters
R Refreshment bars for visiting supporters
T Toilets for visiting supporters

1 A15 London Road
2 Car Parks
3 Peterborough BR Station (1 mile)
4 Glebe Road
5 A605
6 To A1 (north) (5 miles)
7 Main Stand
8 To Whittlesey
9 To A1 (south) (5 miles)
10 Thomas Cook Stand
11 London Road Terrace
12 Moys Terrace (away)

↑ North direction (approx)

▸ 700652
▾ 700662

peterborough united

London Road, Peterborough, PE2 8AL

website: **WWW.THEPOSH.PREMIUMTV.CO.UK**
e:mail: **INFO@THEPOSH.COM**
tel no: **01733 563947**
colours: **BLUE SHIRTS, WHITE SHORTS**
nickname: **POSH**
season 2008/09: **LEAGUE ONE**

With Darren Ferguson, son of Sir Alex, established as manager at Peterborough and with significant investment in the squad, Posh were widely tipped to be amongst the favourites for automatic promotion and in this the team was to prove successful although MK Dons ultimately pipped the team to the League Two championship title. Over the course of the campaign, Posh proved to be free-scoring, hitting no fewer than 84 League goals — a total only exceeded by West Brom in the top four divisions — and conceding only 43. Away from the League, the club showed its potential with a number of impressive cup performances, defeating Championship side Southampton 2-1 at London Road in the 1st round of the Carling Cup and another Championship side, Colchester United, 1-3 away in the 3rd round of the FA Cup. Looking to the new season, the club is undoubtedly ambitious and in Ferguson a manager potentially capable of taking the team further. Although it's perhaps unrealistic to expect the club to challenge for automatic promotion, there must be the outside chance of sneaking into the Play-Offs.

Tel No: 01733 563947
Advance Tickets Tel No: 01733 865674
Fax: 01733 344140
Training Ground: Woodlands, Slash Lane, Castor, Peterborough PE5 7BD
Brief History: Founded in 1934 (no connection with former 'Peterborough and Fletton United' FC). Elected to Football League in 1960. Record attendance 30,096
(Total) Current Capacity: 15,314 (7,669 seated)
Visiting Supporters' Allocation: 4,758 (756 seated)
Nearest Railway Station: Peterborough
Parking (Car): Peterborough
Parking (Coach/Bus): At ground
Police Force and Tel No: Cambridgeshire (01733 563232)
Disabled Visitors' Facilities:
Wheelchairs: South Stand
Blind: No special facility
Future Development(s): The club announced in mid-January 2007 that it was examining the possibility of seeking planning permission to replace the existing terraced Moys End Stand with a new 2,000-seat stand as part of a five-year plan that could ultimately see London Road converted into an all-seater stadium.

season 07/08: League Two **2ND** (promoted) p**46** w**18** d**11** l**17** gf**84** ga**43**

GLEBE ROAD

THOMAS COOK SOUTH STAND
UPPER
DISABLED (D.WING) | LOWER
PITCH SIZE
112 X 71 yards
MOYS TERRACE (COVERED) AWAY
LONDON ROAD TERRACE (COVERED)
LONDON ROAD
ENCLOSURE | DISABLED
A STAND AWAY | MAIN STAND | WEST WING

plymouth argyle

Home Park, Plymouth, PL2 3DQ

website: **WWW.PAFC.PREMIUMTV.CO.UK**
e:mail: **ARGYLE@PAFC.CO.UK**
tel no: **01752 562561**
colours: **WHITE AND GREEN SHIRTS, GREEN SHORTS**
nickname: **THE PILGRIMS**
season 2008/09: **CHAMPIONSHIP**

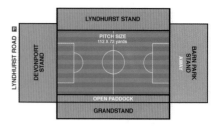

In mid-November, with the club vying for a place in the Play-Offs, it was announced that Ian Holloway, who had been manager at Home Park for just over a year, had resigned, with reports linking him with the managerial vacancy at Leicester City. Following Holloway's departure, the club approached Swindon Town with a view to bringing ex-boss Paul Sturrock back to Home Park, an approach which proved successful. Under Sturrock the team continued to represent one of the teams in the pack chasing the Play-Offs but, with the top half of the Championship a highly competitive environment, the team ultimately finished in 10th place, some six points adrift of the all-important sixth place. As with the Premier League, there would now appear to be a league-within-the-league in the Championship with those teams recently relegated from the top flight having an undoubted advantage in terms of the top six places; there's always a chance that a team like Plymouth — as Hull, Bristol City and Stoke did in 2007/08 — can sneak into these positions but the calibre of the three relegated teams of 2007/08 makes it more difficult. Probably a top-half position with an outside chance of the Play-Offs represent the best that the Home Park fans can expect in the new season.

Advance Tickets Tel No: 0845 338 7232
Fax: 01752 606167
Training Ground: Adjacent to ground
Brief History: Founded 1886 as Argyle Athletic Club, changed name to Plymouth Argyle in 1903. Founder-members Third Division (1920).
Record attendance 43,596

(Total) Current Capacity: 19,500 (all seated)
Visiting Supporters' Allocation: 1,300 (all seated) in Barn Park End Stand up to maximum of 2,000
Nearest Railway Station: Plymouth
Parking (Car): Car park adjacent
Parking (Coach/Bus): Central car park
Police Force and Tel No: Devon & Cornwall (0990 777444)
Disabled Visitors' Facilities:
Wheelchairs: Devonport End
Blind: Commentary available

Anticipated Development(s): Work on the three new stands at Home Park progressed well, with work being completed during the 2001/02 season. Plans, however, for the demolition of the existing Main Stand and its replacement have been resurrected as part of a £37 million redevelopment to create a three-tiered structure taking the ground to 18,600 (all-seated). There is no confirmed timescale for this work.

◄ 701231
▼ 701234

C Club Offices
S Club Shop
E Entrance(s) for visiting
  supporters
R Refreshment bars for visiting
  supporters
T Toilets for visiting supporters

1 Alverstone Road
2 Carisbrook Road
3 A288 Milton Road
4 A2030 Velder Avenue A27
5 A2030 Goldsmith Avenue
6 Fratton BR station
  (½ mile)
7 TY Europe Stand
8 Milton End
9 North Stand
10 South Stand

↑ *North direction (approx)*

▸ 701219
▾ 701226

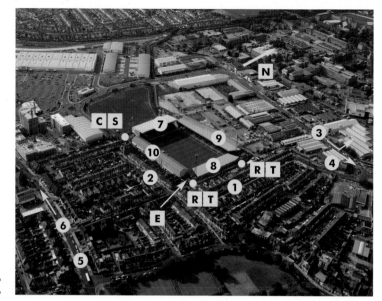

portsmouth

Fratton Park, 57 Frogmore Road, Portsmouth, PO4

website: **WWW.PORTSMOUTHFC.CO.UK**
e:mail: **INFO@POMPEYFC.CO.UK**
tel no: **02392 731204**
colours: **BLUE SHIRTS, WHITE SHORTS**
nickname: **POMPEY**
season 2008/09: **PREMIER LEAGUE**

A season of considerable progress on the field saw Harry Redknapp's Pompey side achieve its highest ever Premier League position — eighth — despite a late run at the end of the campaign when the final four games were lost. This loss of form — which undoubtedly proved a factor in Fulham's ultimate survival — was probably down to one major event — for the first time since 1939, when the club last won the FA Cup (managing to hold on to it for six years, however, courtesy of a certain Adolf Hitler's plans for world domination), Pompey reached the FA Cup Final. In a strange year, none of the supposed teams prospered in the competition resulting in Pompey facing Championship side Cardiff City at Wembley. In an entertaining game, although Cardiff City had the best of the early chances, Kanu eventually sealed Pompey's victory with the only goal of the game just before half time (having previously missed a much easier opportunity). Thus Pompey not only ended the season with silverware, the victory also brings UEFA Cup football to Fratton Park for the first time. For 2008/09, although it's hard to see that the 'Big Four' will perform as lamentably in the cup next season, Pompey under Redknapp should again be challenging for a place in the UEFA Cup courtesy of the League. Probably not strong enough to break into the top four, the team should certainly be capable of competing with Aston Villa and Everton for the top of the also-rans.

Advance Tickets Tel No: 0844 847 1898
Fax: 02392 734129
Club Office: Rodney Road, Portsmouth, PO4 8SX
Training Ground: Stoneham Lane, Eastleigh SO50 9HT
Brief History: Founded 1898. Founder-members Third Division (1920). Record attendance 51,385
(Total) Current Capacity: 20,288 (all seated)
Visiting Supporters' Allocation: 3,121 (max) in Milton Stand
Nearest Railway Station: Fratton
Parking (Car): Street parking
Parking (Coach/Bus): As directed by Police
Police Force and Tel No: Hampshire (02392 321111)
Disabled Visitors' Facilities:
Wheelchairs: TY Europe Stand
Blind: No special facility
Anticipated Development(s): The club's original plans for relocation to a site close to the city's naval dockyard brought objections from the Royal Navy and, as a result, the club identified a new site for the construction of a 36,000-seat ground at Horsea Island. Planning permission for the new ground is to be sought in 2008 with an anticipated completion date of the start of the 2011/12 season. As a temporary measure a roof was installed over the Milton End during the 2007/08 season.

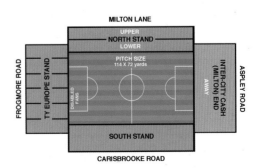

137

port vale

Vale Park, Burslem, Stoke-on-Trent, ST6 1AW
website: **WWW.PORT-VALE.PREMIUMTV.CO.UK**
e:mail: **ENQUIRIES@PORT-VALE.CO.UK**
tel no: **01782 655800**
colours: **WHITE SHIRTS, BLACK SHORTS**
nickname: **THE VALIANTS**
season 2008/09: **LEAGUE TWO**

At the end of September with Port Vale languishing in 23rd position in League One having taken five points from the club's first seven league matches, Martin Foyle departed as manager by mutual consent after just over two years in the job. Following a brief spell with Dean Glover as caretaker, the Valiants appointed Lee Sinnott — who had had considerable success in non-league football taking Farsley Athletic into the Blue Star Premier League — as new manager in early November. However, Sinnott wasn't able to bring a dramatic improvement to the club's position, although there were a number of encouraging results. The team ultimately remained in the League One drop zone throughout the campaign and had it not been for Luton Town having been deducted 10 points for going into Administration, Vale would have finished in 24th place. The team's Achilles Heel was in defence; in the Football League only Accrington Stanley conceded more (mind you, both were overshadowed in the 'leaky defence' syndrome by Premier League Derby who shipped no fewer than 85 goals in eight fewer matches!). Away from the League, Town also suffered the embarrassment of an away defeat at non-league Chasetown in the 2nd round of the FA Cup. As a relegated team, Vale should certainly be amongst the favourites for promotion and the Play-Offs but, as the four teams relegated at the end of 2006/07 proved, League Two can be a struggle and perhaps a near-miss for the Play-Offs is the best that can be expected.

Advance Tickets Tel No: 01782 655832
Fax: 01782 834981
Training Ground: Adjacent to ground
Brief History: Founded 1876 as Burslem Port Vale, changed name to 'Port Vale' in 1907 (reformed club). Former Grounds: The Meadows Longport, Moorland Road Athletic Ground, Cobridge Athletic Grounds, Recreation Ground Hanley, moved to Vale Park in 1950. Founder-members Second Division (1892).
Record attendance 49,768
(Total) Current Capacity: 18,900 (all seated)
Visiting Supporters' Allocation: 4,550
(in Hamil Road [Phones4U] Stand)
Nearest Railway Station: Longport (two miles)
Parking (Car): Car park at Ground
Parking (Coach/Bus): Hamil Road car park
Police Force and Tel No: Staffordshire (01782 577114)
Disabled Visitors' Facilities:
Wheelchairs: 20 spaces in new Britannic Disabled Stand
Blind: Commentary availaable
Anticipated Development(s): After some years of standing half completed, the club's new owners completed the roof over the Lorne Street Stand during the 2004/05 season. The Club had planned to install seats in the remainder of the stand during the 2007/08 season but this is still to be undertaken.

E Entrance(s) for visiting supporters

1 Car Parks
2 Hamil Road
3 Lorne Street
4 To B5051 Moorland Road
5 To Burslem Town Centre
6 Railway Stand
7 Sentinel Stand
8 Hamil Road Stand
9 Lorne Street Stand
10 Family Section

↑ *North direction (approx)*

◀ 700664
▾ 700669

▲ 700985
▶ 700977

S Club Shop

1 A6033 Deepdale Road
2 Lawthorpe Road
3 Car Park
4 A5085 Blackpool Road
5 Preston BR Station
(2 miles)
6 Bill Shankly Stand
7 Tom Finney Stand
8 Town End Stand
9 Invincibles Stand

⬆ *North direction (approx)*

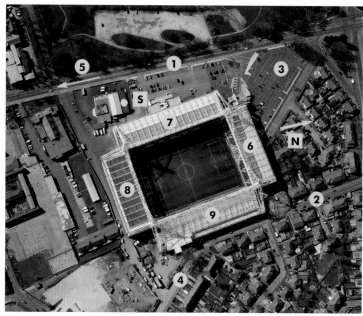

preston north end

Deepdale, Sir Tom Finney Way, Preston, PR1 6RU

website: **WWW.PNEFC.PREMIUMTV.CO.UK**
e:mail: **ENQUIRIES@PNE.COM**
tel no: **0870 442 1964**
colours: **WHITE SHIRTS, BLUE SHORTS**
nickname: **THE LILYWHITES**
season 2008/09: **CHAMPIONSHIP**

Football is a fickle game. Despite having led Preston almost into the Premier League at the end of the 2006/07 season, a poor start to the 2007/08 season, culminating in a 3-0 defeat at Hull City that left the club in 21st position in the League Championship, Paul Simpson was sacked as manager in mid-November with assistant Rob Kelly taking over as caretaker. The club appointed Alan Irvine, previously the assistant coach at Everton, to replace him. Under Irvine the club cemented its League Championship status, ultimately finishing in 15th place some four points above relegated Leicester City. Away from the League, the club suffered the embarrassment of a 2-1 home defeat by League Two side Morecambe in the 1st round of the Carling Cup — the first season in which Morecambe had played in the competition. For 2008/09, with competition at both ends of the table likely to be highly tight, Irvine's team should have the potential to achieve a top-half finish although promotion and the Play-Offs look unlikely.

Advance Tickets Tel No: 0870 4421966
Fax: 01772 693366
Training Ground: Springfields Sports Ground, Dodney Drive, Lea, Preston PR2 1XR
Brief History: Founded 1867 as a Rugby Club, changed to soccer in 1881. Former ground: Moor Park, moved to (later named) Deepdale in 1875. Founder-members Football League (1888). Record attendance 42,684
(Total) Current Capacity: 22,225 (all seated)
Visiting Supporters' Allocation: 6,000 maximum in Bill Shankly Stand
Nearest Railway Station: Preston (2 miles)
Parking (Car): West Stand car park
Parking (Coach/Bus): West Stand car park
Police Force and Tel No: Lancashire (01772 203203)
Disabled Visitors' Facilities:
Wheelchairs: Tom Finney Stand and Bill Shankly Stand
Blind: Earphones Commentary
Anticipated Development(s): Work started on the redevelopment of the fourth side of the ground in 2007. The new structure, destined to replace the Pavilion Stand of the 1930s and is due to be named the Invincibles Stand in honour of the double-winning side of 1888/1889. The stand, which will cost some £6 million, will provide seating for 4,500 along with executive boxes, taking the ground's capacity to 24,000.

season 07/08: Championship **15TH** p46 **w15** d11 **l20** gf50 **ga56**

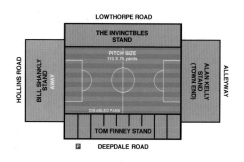

LOWTHORPE ROAD

THE INVINCTBLES STAND

PITCH SIZE
110 X 75 yards

HOLLINS ROAD

BILL SHANKLY STAND AWAY

ALAN KELLY STAND (TOWN END)

ALLEYWAY

DISABLED FANS

TOM FINNEY STAND

DEEPDALE ROAD

queens park rangers

Loftus Road Stadium, South Africa Road, London, W12 7PA

website: **WWW.QPR.PREMIUMTV.CO.UK**
e:mail: **BOXOFFICE@QPR.CO.UK**
tel no: **020 8743 0262**
colours: **BLUE AND WHITE HOOPED SHIRTS, WHITE SHORTS**
nickname: **THE SUPERHOOPS**
season 07/08: **CHAMPIONSHIP**

All change at Loftus Road in the early part of the season as new owners — led by Formula 1 supremo Bernie Eccleston — moved into the boardroom and John Gregory moved out of the managerial office. This took place towards the end of September following a run of seven League games without a win that left Rangers adrift at the bottom of the League Championship table, at which point Mick Harford took over as caretaker boss. The new owners moved quickly and appointed Luigi de Canio as the team's new manager but the new boss's tenure was destined to be short-lived as, having guided the team to 14th place, De Canio left at the end of the season. His replacement, the well-travelled and experienced Iain Dowie, will have the advantage of significant money behind him, courtesy of the club's new owners, but that will undoubtedly raise the level of expectation accordingly.

Advance Tickets Tel No: 0844 477 7007
Fax: 020 8749 0994
Training Ground: Imperial College Sports Ground, Sipson Lane, Harlington, Middlesex UB3 5AQ
Brief History: Founded 1885 as 'St. Jude's Institute', amalgamated with Christchurch Rangers to become Queens Park Rangers in 1886. Football League record number of former Grounds and Ground moves (13 different venues, 17 changes), including White City Stadium (twice). Final move to Loftus Road in 1963. Founder-members Third Division (1920). Record attendance (at Loftus Road) 35,353
(Total) Current Capacity: 19,130 (all seated)
Visiting Supporters' Allocation: 2,500 (maximum)
Nearest Railway Station: Shepherds Bush and White City (both tube)
Parking (Car): White City NCP and street parking
Parking (Coach/Bus): White City NCP
Police Force and Tel No: Metropolitan (020 8741 6212)
Disabled Visitors' Facilities:
Wheelchairs: Ellerslie Road Stand and West Paddock
Blind: Ellerslie Road Stand
Anticipated Development(s): There is vague talk of possible relocation, but nothing has been confirmed.
Given the constrained site occupied by Loftus Road, it will be difficult to increase the existing ground's capacity.

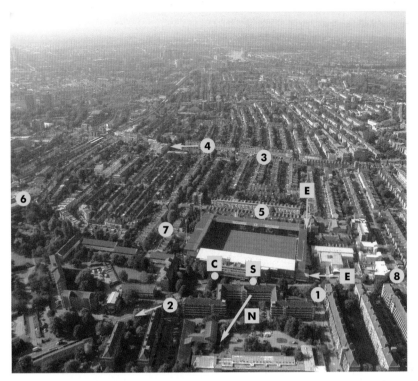

C Club Offices
S Club Shop
E Entrance(s) for visiting
  supporters

1 South Africa Road
2 To White City Tube Station,
  A219 Wood Lane and A40
  Western Avenue
3 A4020 Uxbridge Road
4 To Shepherds Bush Tube
  Station
5 Ellerslie Road
6 BBC Television Centre
7 Loftus Road
8 Bloemfontein Road

↑ *North direction (approx)*

◄ 700895
▼ 700889

143

C Club Offices
S Club Shop

1 North Stand
2 East Stand
3 South Stand (away)
4 West Stand
5 A33 Basingstoke Road
6 A33 to M4 (Jct 11)
7 A33 to Reading Town Centre
   and station (two miles)
8 Hurst Way
9 Boot End

⬆ *North direction (approx)*

▸ 699828
▾ 699833

144

reading

Madejski Stadium, Bennet Road, Reading, RG2 0FL

website: **WWW.READINGFC.PREMIUMTV.CO.UK**
e:mail: **CUSTOMERSERVICE@READINGFC.CO.UK**
tel no: **0118 968 1100**
colours: **WHITE WITH BLUE HOOPS SHIRTS, WHITE SHORTS**
nickname: **THE ROYALS**
season 2008/09: **CHAMPIONSHIP**

Having surprised many by achieving a top-half finish at the end of the 2006/07 season, Reading were looking to consolidate their position in the top flight in 2007/08. However, the club suffered a severe bout of 'second seasonitis' and struggled throughout much of the campaign to stay out of the relegation battle. A bad period midway through the season seemed to indicate that the club was in freefall, but a spirited effort in February and March seemed to suggest that Steve Coppell's team had weathered the storm and was capable of surviving. However, a poor run at the end of the season that saw the club fail to score in six successive games in April and May, gaining only two points in the period, saw them enter the final game of the season — away at already doomed Derby County — knowing that a win was essential and hoping that Fulham would fail to win at Portsmouth. Reading did their bit — scoring an easy 4-0 victory at Pride Park — but the Cottagers' late winner at Fratton Park means that Reading will return to the Championship after two years. Steve Coppell remains in charge of the reins at the Madejski Stadium in 2008/09 but a number of players will have departed as a result of relegation; still, the parachute payments will ensure that the team has the financial muscle to attempt a serious push back to the top flight. Reading will be one of the pre-season favourites to make an immediate return and the club should certainly have the ability to make the Play-Offs at least.

Advance Tickets Tel No: 0870 999 1871
Fax: 0118 968 1101
Training Ground: Reading FC Academy Training Ground, Hogwood Lane, Arborfield Garrison, Wokingham RG40 4QW
Brief History: Founded 1871. Amalgamated with Reading Hornets in 1877 and with Earley in 1889. Former Grounds: Reading Recreation Ground, Reading Cricket Ground, Coley Park, Caversham Cricket Cround and Elm Park (1895-1998); moved to the Madejski Stadium at the start of the 1998/99 season. Founder-members of the Third Division in 1920. Record attendance (at Elm Park) 33,042; (at Madejski Stadium) 24,122
(Total) Current Capacity: 24,200 (all seated)
Visiting Supporters' Allocation: 4,500 (maximum in the Fosters Lager South Stand)
Nearest Railway Station: Reading (2.5 miles)
Parking (Car): 1,800-space car park at the ground, 700 of these spaces are reserved
Parking (Coach/Bus): As directed
Other Clubs Sharing Ground: London Irish RUFC
Police Force and Tel No: Thames Valley (0118 953 6000)
Disabled Visitors' Facilities:
Wheelchairs: 128 designated spaces on all four sides of the ground
Blind: 12 places for match day commentaries
Anticipated Development(s): The club applied for Planning Permission to expand the capacity of the Madejski Stadium by 14,000 seats in October 2005, taking the ground's capacity up from 24,000 to 38,000. Permission was subsequently granted and will involve extending the North, South and East stands. Work is scheduled to start in the summer of 2008 with an anticipated completion date of the end of 2009.

season 07/08: FA Premier League **18TH** (relegated) **p38 w10 d6 l22 gf41 ga66**

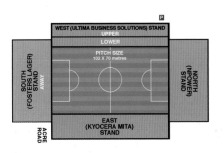

rochdale

Spotland Stadium, Willbutts Lane, Rochdale, OL11 5DS

website: **WWW.ROCHDALEAFC.PREMIUMTV.CO.UK**
e:mail: **OFFICE@ROCHDALEAFC.CO.UK**
tel no: **0870 822 1907**
colours: **BLUE SHIRTS, BLUE SHORTS**
nickname: **THE DALE**
season 2008/09: **LEAGUE TWO**

season 07/08: League Two **5TH p46 w23 d11 l12 gf77 ga54**

Having played in the lowest tier of the English League for some four decades, Rochdale holds the record as the longest surviving team at this level but, for much of the 2007/08 season, it looked as though The Dale might have been capable of finally making a break. Although never seriously in the hunt for automatic promotion, the club was to achieve a Play-Off place. A 2-1 victory in the northeast seemed to have given Darlington the edge but Dale's 1-0 victory at Spotland sent the game into extra time and, despite being reduced to 10 men, Dale scored twice more to set up a final at Wembley against Stockport. Although taking an early lead, Rochdale were eventually to lose 3-2 resulting in the promised land of promotion being missed again. Keith Hill has shown in his time as Rochdale's manager that he's capable of building a team to challenge for promotion and, with a number of financially-weakened teams being relegated, 2008/09 could be Dale's best chance to achieve a top-three position although the Play-Offs remain a more realistic aim again.

Advance Tickets Tel No: 0870 822 1907
Fax: 01706 648466
Training Ground: No specific facility
Brief History: Founded 1907 from former Rochdale Town F.C. (founded 1900). Founder-members Third Division North (1921). Record attendance 24,231
(Total) Current Capacity: 10,262 (8,342 seated)
Visiting Supporters' Allocation: 3,650 (seated) in Willbutts Lane (Westrose Leisure) Stand
Nearest Railway Station: Rochdale
Parking (Car): Rear of ground
Parking (Coach/Bus): Rear of ground
Other Clubs Sharing Ground: Rochdale Hornets RLFC
Police Force and Tel No: Greater Manchester (0161 872 5050)
Disabled Visitors' Facilities:
Wheelchairs: Main, WMG and Willbutts Lane stands – disabled area
Blind: Commentary available
Anticipated Development(s): None following completion of Willbutts Lane Stand.

Courtesy of Rochdale Football Club

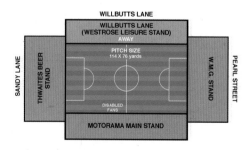

WILLBUTTS LANE

WILLBUTTS LANE
(WESTROSE LEISURE STAND)
AWAY

PITCH SIZE
114 X 76 yards

SANDY LANE

THWAITES BEER STAND

DISABLED FANS

W.M.G. STAND

PEARL STREET

MOTORAMA MAIN STAND

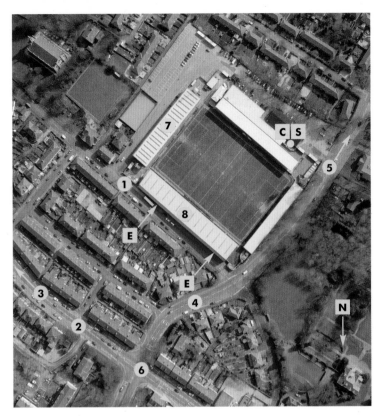

C Club Offices
S Club Shop
E Entrance(s) for visiting
  supporters

1 Willbutts Lane
2 A627 Edenfield Road
3 Rochdale BR Station
  (½ mile)
4 Sandy Lane
5 To M62
6 To M65 and North
7 Pearl Street (Westrose Leisure)
  Stand
8 Willbutts Lane Stand

↑ *North direction (approx)*

◄ 696966
▼ 696972

E Entrance(s) for visiting supporters

1 B6085 Darnall Road
2 A6178 Attercliffe Road
3 To Arena/Don Valley Stadium Supertram stop (one mile)
4 To Attercliffe Supertram stop (one mile)
5 B6083 Newhall Road
6 Worksop Road
7 To A6012 and Darnall railway station (two miles)
8 To Sheffield city centre and main line railway station (2½ miles)
9 To M1 Junction 34 (South) (1½ miles)
10 To Rotherham town centre (four miles)
11 Supertram route and freight-only railway line

↑ North direction (approx)

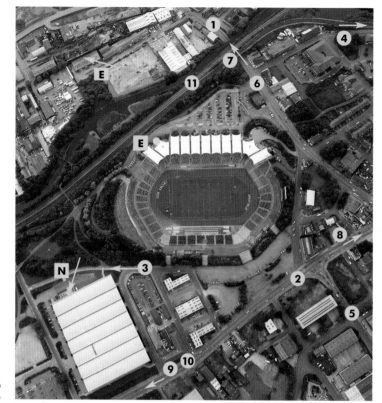

▸ 701360
▾ 701366

148

rotherham united

Don Valley Stadium, Worksop Road, Sheffield, S9 3TL

website: **WWW.THEMILLERS.PREMIUMTV.CO.UK**
e:mail: **OFFICE@ROTHERHAMUNITED.NET**
tel no: **0871 423 1884***
colours: **RED SHIRTS, WHITE SHORTS**
nickname: **THE MILLERS**
season 2008/09: **LEAGUE TWO**

Relegated at the end of the 2007/08 season, Mark Robins' team seemed to be making a decent bid to challenge for a Play-Off place when the financial troubles that had beset the club before resurfaced and the Millers were once again placed into Administration. The automatic 10-point deduction all but scuppered the team's chances of reaching even the Play-Offs and, following the deduction, the team's form slipped. However, a late return to form saw the team ultimately finish in a creditable 9th place although, even if the 10 points hadn't been deducted, the club would just have missed out on a Play-Off place. At the time of writing, United had just emerged from Administration following severe doubts as to whether the club would survive. With the uncertainty, Robins will be under a distinct disadvantage in terms of trying to maintain and build a squad for the new season. As other clubs — such as now-relegated Wrexham have found — this is an almost impossible situation and, unless the club's position is speedily resolved, it's hard to escape the conclusion that the battles of 2007/08 to ensure the club's survival will be replicated on the field in 2008/09 to retain League status.

Advance Tickets Tel No: 01709 512760*
Fax: 01709 512762*
* These numbers apply to Millmoor and will probably change with the club's relocation.
Training Ground: Hooton Training Ground, Thomas Street, Kilnhurst, Mexborough S64 5TF
Brief History: Founded 1877 (as Thornhill, later Thornhill United), changed name to Rotherham County in 1905 and to Rotherham United in 1925 (amalgamated with Rotherham Town — Football League members 1893-97 — in 1925). Former Grounds include Red House Ground and Clifton Lane Cricket Ground, moved to Millmoor in 1907 and to the Don Valley Stadium in 2008. Record attendance (at Millmoor): 25,170
(Total) Current Capacity: 25,000 (all seated)
Visiting Supporters' Allocation: tbc
Nearest Railway Station: Arena/River Don Stadium stop on Sheffield Supertram network is 100m from the ground; Sheffield Supertram provides a link between the two nearest main line stations — Sheffield (two miles approx) and Meadowhall (1.5 miles approx)
Parking (Car): As directed
Parking (Coach/Bus): As directed
Other Clubs Sharing Ground: Sheffield Eagles RLFC
Police Force and Tel No: South Yorkshire (01709 371121)
Disabled Visitors' Facilities:
Wheelchairs: 12 wheelchair spaces
Blind: No special facility
Anticipated Development(s): Problems with occupation of the club's existing ground at Millmoor as a result of the process of bringing the club out of Administration and its acquisition by Tony Stewart led to the club leaving Millmoor during the summer of 2008 and relocating to the Don Valley Stadium. The club is hoping to work with Rotherham Council to develop a new community stadium in the town.

*10 points deducted for going into Administration again

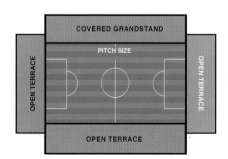

149

scunthorpe united

Glanford Park, Doncaster Road, Scunthorpe, DN15 8TD

website: **WWW.SCUNTHORPE–UNITED.PREMIUMTV.CO.UK**
e:mail: **ADMIN@SCUNTHORPE–UNITED.CO.UK**
tel no: **0871 221 1899**
colours: **CLARET AND BLUE SHIRTS, CLARET SHORTS**
nickname: **THE IRON**
season 2008/09: **LEAGUE ONE**

Promoted as League One champions at the end of the 2006/07 season, it was always going to be a challenge for Scunthorpe United to prosper at the higher level and the team was rooted in the relegation zone for much of the campaign. With relegation confirmed well before the end of the season, Nigel Adkins' team was ultimately to finish in 23rd position. Not only did the League prove difficult, the team also had limited success in the Carling Cup, losing to League One side Hartlepool United at home 2-1 in the 1st round. For 2008/09, as one of the relegated teams, Scunthorpe ought to be amongst the pre-season favourites to make an immediate return either via automatic promotion or via the Play-Offs but as teams such as Nottingham Forest have shown, success is by no means guaranteed and a Play-Off place is perhaps the best that can be hoped for.

Advance Tickets Tel No: 0871 221 1899
Fax: 01724 857986
Training Ground: Grange Farm, Neap House Road, Gunness, Scunthorpe DN15 8TX
Brief History: Founded 1899 as Scunthorpe United, amalgamated with North Lindsey to become 'Scunthorpe & Lindsey United' in 1912. Changed name to Scunthorpe United in 1956. Former Grounds: Crosby (Lindsey United) and Old Showground, moved to Glanford Park in 1988. Elected to Football League in 1950. Record attendance 8,906 (23,935 at Old Showground)
(Total) Current Capacity: 9,200 (6,400 seated)
Visiting Supporters' Allocation: 1,678 (all seated) in South (Caparo Merchant Bar) Stand
Nearest Railway Station: Scunthorpe
Parking (Car): At ground
Parking (Coach/Bus): At ground
Police Force and Tel No: Humberside (01724 282888)
Disabled Visitors' Facilities:
Wheelchairs: County Chef Stand
Blind: Commentary available

Anticipated Development(s): The club is seeking planning permission to redevelop the North (Study United) Stand at Glandford Park with the intention of increasing the ground's capacity to 11,000. If consent is granted work should start during 2008. In addition, the club is also looking at the possibility of a further relocation, although nothing is confirmed at the present time.

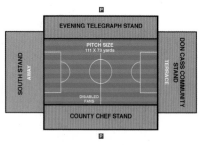

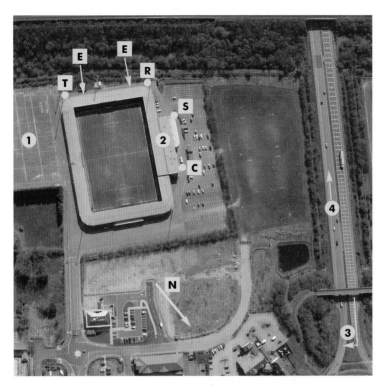

C Club Offices
S Club Shop
E Entrance(s) for visiting
   supporters
R Refreshment bars for visiting
   supporters
T Toilets for visiting supporters

1 Car Park
2 Evening Telegraph Stand
3 A18 to Scunthorpe BR Station
   and Town Centre (1 1/2 miles)
4 M181 and
   M180 Junction 3

↑ North direction (approx)

◀ 700699
▼ 700707

C Club Offices
S Club Shop
E Entrance(s) for visiting
supporters

1 A621 Bramall Lane
2 Shoreham Street
3 Car Park
4 Sheffield Midland BR Station
(¼ mile)
5 John Street
6 Hallam FM (Kop) Stand
7 John Street Stand
8 Bramall Lane
(Gordon Lamb) Stand
9 Laver (South) Stand

↑ *North direction (approx)*

▸ 701102
▾ 701110

sheffield united

Bramall Lane, Sheffield, S2 4SU

website: **WWW.SUFC.PREMIUMTV.CO.UK**
e:mail: **INFO@SUFC.CO.UK**
tel no: **0871 222 1899**
colours: **RED AND WHITE STRIPED SHIRTS, BLACK SHORTS**
nickname: **THE BLADES**
season 2008/09: **CHAMPIONSHIP**

Following the disappointment of relegation — in controversial circumstances — from the Premier League at the end of the 2006/07 season and following Neil Warnock's decision to stand down, new manager Bryan Robson was widely expected to lead the team back towards the top division. As a manager, Robson has had both success — with Middlesbrough — and failure — as ultimately with West Brom — and at Bramall Lane his career was to be relatively short-lived as the team failed to offer a serious challenge in the early months of the campaign. Sidelined in mid-February, after his team won only 14 games out of 39 following a 0-0 draw with relegation-threatened Scunthorpe United that left the Blades in 16th place, seven points above the drop zone, Robson, who declined an alternative job with the club, was replaced by Kevin Blackwell. Blackwell, popular having been at the club earlier in his career, thus made an immediate return to football after his departure from Luton Town. Under Blackwell the Blades made significant progress and retained a mathematical — but slim — hope of a Play-Off place even on the final Sunday. Finishing ninth was a distinct improvement on what had seemed likely earlier and offers an excellent platform for a more sustained push in 2008/09 — the last of the club's two-year parachute payments. Outside the League, one of the season's high points was the victory over Manchester City in the FA Cup where the goal should probably have been credited to 'A. Balloon' — one of the more surreal goals to be seen during the 2007/08 season.

Advance Tickets Tel No: 0871 222 1889
Fax: 0871 663 2430
Training Ground: The Hallam FM Academy @ Sheffield United, 614A Firshill Crescent, Sheffield S4 7DJ
Brief History: Founded 1889. (Sheffield Wednesday occasionally used Bramall Lane c1880.) Founder-members 2nd Division (1892). Record attendance 68,287
(Total) Current Capacity: 33,000 (all seated)
Visiting Supporters' Allocation: 3,000 (seated) can be increased to 5,200 if needed
Nearest Railway Station: Sheffield Midland
Parking (Car): Street parking
Parking (Coach/Bus): As directed by Police
Police Force and Tel No: South Yorkshire (0114 276 8522)
Disabled Visitors' Facilities:
Wheelchairs: South Stand
Blind: Commentary available
Anticipated Development(s): The club has plans for the expansion of the Kop Stand adding 3,000 to Bramall Lane's capacity and to the South Stand adding 4,000, giving the ground a new total capacity of 40,000. There is no confirmed timescale for the work although it could start later in 2008.

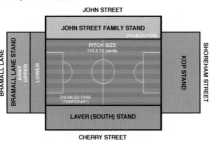

JOHN STREET

JOHN STREET FAMILY STAND

DISABLED FANS

BRAMALL LANE STAND
AWAY UPPER
LOWER

PITCH SIZE
113 X 72 yards

SHOREHAM STREET
KOP STAND

DISABLED FANS (TEMPORARY)

LAVER (SOUTH) STAND

CHERRY STREET

sheffield wednesday

Hillsborough, Sheffield, S6 1SW

website: **WWW.SWFC.PREMIUMTV.CO.UK**
e:mail: **ENQUIRIES@SWFC.CO.UK**
tel no: **0870 999 1867**
colours: **BLUE AND WHITE STRIPED SHIRTS, BLACK SHORTS**
nickname: **THE OWLS**
season 2008/09: **CHAMPIONSHIP**

In one of the tightest relegation battles seen for many years, Brian Laws' Sheffield Wednesday outfit was to finish in 16th position but only three points off the drop zone and, if results had gone other ways, it could have been the Owls joining Colchester and Scunthorpe in League One. No fewer than five teams — Blackpool, Coventry, Leicester and Southampton along with Wednesday — could all mathematically have gone down but of all the teams threatened, Wednesday achieved the most emphatic escape courtesy of a 4-1 victory at Hillsborough over Norwich City. Currently the Owls seem to perform strongly in alternate seasons; relegation threatened one year and promotion candidates the next. On this basis the team should be one of those chasing a Play-Off place in 2008/09 but the reality is probably that a position of mid-table safety beckons.

Advance Tickets Tel No: 0871 230 1867
Fax: 0114 221 2122
Training Ground: Sheffield Wednesday Football Club Training Ground, Middlewood Road, Sheffield, S6 4HA
Brief History: Founded 1867 as The Wednesday F.C. (changed to Sheffield Wednesday c1930). Former Grounds: London Road, Wyrtle Road (Heeley), Sheaf House Ground, Encliffe & Olive Grove (Bramall Lane also used occasionally), moved to Hillsborough (then named 'Owlerton' in 1899). Founder-members Second Division (1892). Record attendance 72,841
(Total) Current Capacity: 39,859 (all seated)
Visiting Supporters' Allocation: 3,700 (all seated) in West Stand Upper
Nearest Railway Station: Sheffield (2 miles)
Parking (Car): Street Parking
Parking (Coach/Bus): Owlerton Stadium
Police Force and Tel No: South Yorkshire (0114 276 8522)
Disabled Visitors' Facilities:
Wheelchairs: North and Lower West Stands
Blind: Commentary available

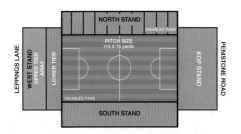

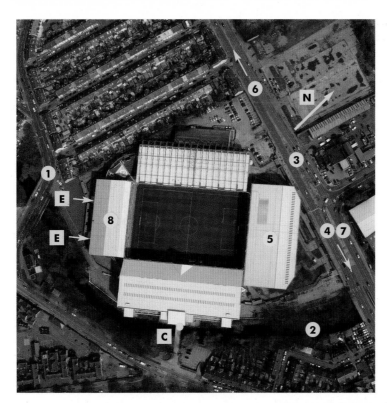

C Club Offices
E Entrance(s) for visiting
 supporters

1 Leppings Lane
2 River Don
3 A61 Penistone Road North
4 Sheffield BR Station and City
 Centre (2 miles)
5 Spion Kop
6 To M1 (North)
7 To M1 (South)
8 West Stand

↑ North direction (approx)

◀ 701078
▾ 701082

1 B4380 Oteley Road
2 Meole Brace roundabout
3 Shrewsbury–Hereford railway
  line
4 To Shrewsbury station
  (two miles)
5 A5112 Hereford Road to A5
  (ring road)
6 A5191 Hereford Road to
  town centre and railway
  station
7 Footpath under railway to
  retail park
8 North Stand (away)

↑ North direction (approx)

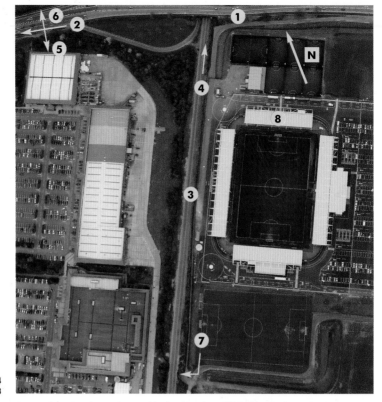

▸ 701114
▾ 701118

shrewsbury town

New Stadium, Oteley Road, Shrewsbury, SY2 6ST

website: **WWW.SHREWSBURYTOWN.PREMIUMTV.CO.UK**
e:mail: **IAN@SHREWSBURYTOWN.CO.UK**
tel no: **0871 811 8800**
colours: **BLUE SHIRTS, BLUE SHORTS**
nickname: **THE SHREWS**
season 2008/09: **LEAGUE TWO**

A season of some promise at Shrewsbury — a new ground and making the Play-Off final at Wembley at the end of the 2006/07 season — started well with the Shrews amongst the early pace-makers. However, the team's form was not to be sustained and as the team gradually drifted down the League Two table so the level of discontent amongst the fans grew. Following a poor run of form, Gary Peters departed as manager in early March and the club moved quickly to appoint Paul Simpson, the ex-boss at Preston, to the full-time position. Well experienced in football at this level, Simpson arrived too late in the campaign to achieve a dramatic reversal in fortune for the club and 18th position was ultimately a considerable disappointment. With the season over, Simpson is likely to institute a considerable overhaul of the squad and Town should certainly be capable of improving on their 2007/08 standing in 2008/09. One thing missing from the new season, however, will be local derbies against Wrexham; relegation for the Welsh side to the Blue Star Premier League was all but confirmed by the 3-0 defeat at Town.

Advance Tickets Tel No: 01743 273943
Fax: 0871 811 8801
Training Ground: Sundorne Castle training Ground, Newport Road, Sundorne, Shrewsbury SY1 4RR
Brief History: Founded 1886. Former Grounds: Monkmoor Racecourse, Ambler's Field; The Barracks Ground and the Gay Meadow (1910-2007); moved to the new ground for start of 2007/08 season. Elected to Football League 1950; relegated to Nationwide Conference at end of 2002/03 and promoted back to the Football league, via the Play-Offs, at the end of 2003/04. Record attendance at Gay Meadow 18,917; at the New Stadium 8,753
(Total) Current Capacity: 10,000 (all seated)
Visiting Supporters' Allocation: tbc (North Stand)
Nearest Railway Station: Shrewsbury (two miles)
Parking (Car): at ground
Parking (Coach/Bus): at ground
Police Force and Tel No: West Mercia (01743 232888)
Disabled Visitors' Facilities:
Wheelchairs: c40 spaces in North (away), South and East stands
Blind: Commentary available
Anticipated Development(s): The club successfully moved into the New Meadow for the start of the 2007/08 season. During the summer of 2007 the old Gay Meadow was demolished prior to the site being redeveloped for housing. The new ground is designed to permit the construction of corner stands should the need arise.

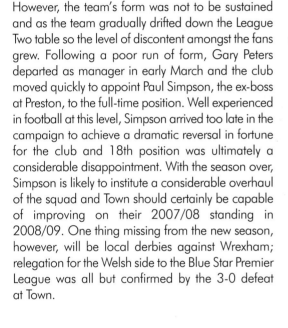

southampton

St Mary's Stadium, Britannia Road, Southampton, SO14 5FP

website: **WWW.SAINTSFC.CO.UK**
e:mail: **SFC@SAINTSFC.CO.UK**
tel no: **0845 688 94448**
colours: **RED AND WHITE SHIRTS, BLACK SHORTS**
nickname: **THE SAINTS**
season 07/08: **CHAMPIONSHIP**

Overall the 2007/08 season will not go down as one of the most successful in Southampton's history as the club's Championship status came into serious question. Following Alex McLeish's decision to take over as manager of Birmingham City, George Burley was appointed Scotland manager in mid-January 2008. Nigel Pearson took over as manager in mid-February having departed from Newcastle United following the arrival of Kevin Keegan. Come the last day of the season, however, Southampton were firmly rooted in the bottom three but were one of five teams — the others being Blackpool, Coventry, Leicester and Sheffield Wednesday — that could all face the drop if results went against them. The Saints' position was, moreover, handicapped further by having the worst goal difference of the five, a factor that might have proved crucial. In the event, however, a 3-2 victory over Sheffield United at home coupled with results elsewhere meant that Leicester were relegated and Saints survived to battle another year in the Championship. The club also struggled in the cups, losing away at Peterborough United 2-1 in the 1st round of the Carling Cup and at Hereford United in the 2nd round of the FA Cup 2-0. Of the five teams battling it out, three were sides that had fallen out of the Premier League and had subsequently lost the parachute payments, emphasising how teams such as Southampton can quickly become also-rans. It's hard to escape the conclusion that 2008/09 may well be another season of struggle for the Saints, now managed by Jan Poortvliet following the departure of Nigel Pearson at the end of the season, and that even a Play-Off place looks beyond them.

Advance Tickets Tel No: 0845 688 9288
Fax: 0845 688 9445
Training Ground: Staplewood, Club House, Long Lane, Marchwood, Southampton SO40 4WR
Brief History: Founded 1885 as 'Southampton St. Mary's Young Men's Association (changed name to Southampton in 1897). Former Grounds: Northlands Road, Antelope Ground, County Ground, moved to The Dell in 1898 and to St Mary's Stadium in 2001. Founder members Third Division (1920). Record attendance (at The Dell) 31,044 (at St Mary's) 32,151
(Total) Current Capacity: 32,689 (all seated)
Visiting Supporters' Allocation: c3,200 in Northam Stand (can be increased to 4,750 if required)
Nearest Railway Station: Southampton Central
Parking (Car): Street parking or town centre car parks
Parking (Coach/Bus): As directed by the police
Police Force and Tel No: Hampshire (02380 335444)
Disabled Visitors' Facilities:
Wheelchairs: c200 places
Blind: Commentary available
Anticipated Development(s): Following completion of the new stadium the club has no further plans at present.

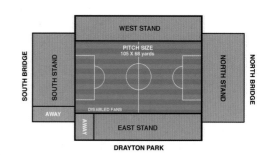

C Club Offices
S Club Shop
E Entrance(s) for visiting supporters

1 A3024 Northam Road
2 B3028 Britannia Road
3 River Itchen
4 To M27 (five miles)
5 To Southampton Central station and town centre
6 Marine Parade
7 To A3025 (and Itchen toll bridge)
8 Belvedere Road
9 North Stand

↑ North direction (approx)

◄ 701369
▼ 701374

C Club Offices

E Entrance(s) for visiting supporters

R Refreshment bars for visiting supporters

T Toilets for visiting supporters

1 Director's Car Park

2 Prittlewell BR Station (¼ mile)

3 A127 Victoria Aveneue

4 Fairfax Drive

5 Southend centre (½ mile)

6 North (Universal Cycles) Stand

↑ North direction (approx)

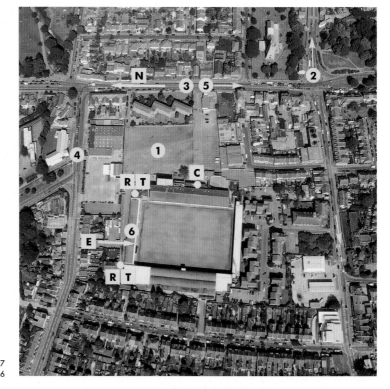

▸ 697297
▾ 697286

southend united

Roots Hall, Victoria Avenue, Southend-on-Sea, SS2 6NQ

website: **WWW.SOUTHENDUNITED.PREMIUMTV.CO.UK**
e:mail: **INFO@SOUTHEND-UNITED.CO.UK**
tel no: **01702 304050**
colours: **BLUE SHIRTS, BLUE SHORTS**
nickname: **THE SHRIMPERS**
season 2008/09: **LEAGUE ONE**

Relegated at the end of the 2006/07 season from the Championship, Steve Tilson's team were one of those widely considered at the start of the new season as being amongst those capable of making a swift return. Although the team was never one of those capable of sustaining a serious challenge for one of the two automatic spots, the team did secure a Play-Off place and thus the possibility of a return to the Championship via Wembley. However, a 0-0 draw with Doncaster Rovers at Roots Hall combined with a 5-1 defeat at the Keepmoat Stadium meant that the League One Play-Off final was an all-Yorkshire affair and Southend was consigned to a further year in League One. In the new season local rivalry with relegated Colchester United is renewed with both vying to make a return to the Championship. United should again have the potential to be one of the clubs in the hunt for a Play-Off berth at best.

Advance Tickets Tel No: 0844 477 0077
Fax: 01702 304124
Training Ground: Eastern Avenue, Southend-on-Sea SS2 4DX
Brief History: Founded 1906. Former Grounds: Roots Hall, Kursaal, the Stadium Grainger Road, moved to Roots Hall (new Ground) 1955. Founder-members Third Division (1920). Record attendance 31,033
(Total) Current Capacity: 12,392 (all seated)
Visiting Supporters' Allocation: 2,700 (maximum) (all seated) in North Stand and North West Enclosure
Nearest Railway Station: Prittlewell
Parking (Car): Street parking
Parking (Coach/Bus): Car park at Ground
Police Force and Tel No: Essex (01702 431212)
Disabled Visitors' Facilities:
Wheelchairs: West Stand
Blind: Commentary available
Anticipated Development(s): The club submitted a proposal for the construction of its new £50 million 22,000-seat ground at Fossetts Farm to the council in early October 2006 and formal consent was granted by the council in January 2007 although this was subject to a public inquiry. Formal approval for the work was granted in March 2008. The new ground, designed by HOK (who also designed the Emirates Stadium), is scheduled for completion by the start of the 2010/11 season.

stockport county

Edgeley Park, Hardcastle Road, Edgeley, Stockport, SK3 9DD

website: **WWW.STOCKPORTCOUNTY.PREMIUMTV.CO.UK**
e:mail: **FANS@STOCKPORTCOUNTY.COM**
tel no: **0161 286 8888**
colours: **BLUE AND WHITE STRIPED SHIRTS, BLUE SHORTS**
nickname: **THE HATTERS**
season 2008/09: **LEAGUE ONE**

season 07/08: League Two **4TH** (promoted) p**46** w**24** d**10** l**12** gf**72** ga**54**

One of the teams in the pack chasing the top three, Stockport County under Jim Gannon ultimately lost out in the race to achieve one of the automatic promotion places but, in finishing fourth, the club was to set up a Play-Off semi-final against Wycombe Wanderers. A 1-1 draw at Adams Park combined with a 1-0 victory at home sent County through to a Wembley showdown with Rochdale. Although Rochdale took an early lead, County were to prove the stronger outfit and ultimately ran out 3-2 winners. Away from the League, the club was to suffer an embarrassing defeat on penalties at non-league Staines Town in a FA Cup first round replay following a 1-1 draw at Edgeley Park; conversely, however, in the Carling Cup 1st round the Hatters won a 1-0 victory at home over League One Tranmere Rovers. As a result of the Play-Off victory, League One football returns to Edgeley Park in 2008/09; as a team promoted through the Play-Offs, County will undoubtedly be one of the pre-season favourites for the drop but the lower echelons of League One has a number of relatively weak teams and, if the season starts well, then the team should survive at this higher level.

Advance Tickets Tel No: 0845 688 5799
Fax: 0161 286 8900
Training Ground: Details omitted at club's request
Brief History: Founded 1883 as Heaton Norris Rovers, changed name to Stockport County in 1890. Former Grounds: Heaton Norris Recreation Ground, Heaton Norris Wanderers Cricket Ground, Chorlton's Farm, Ash Inn Ground, Wilkes Field (Belmont Street) and Nursery Inn (Green Lane), moved to Edgeley Park in 1902. Record attendance 27,833
(Total) Current Capacity: 11,000 (all seated)
Visiting Supporters' Allocation: 800 (all seated) in Vernon Stand (can be increased by 1,500 all-seated on open Railway End if needed)
Nearest Railway Station: Stockport
Parking (Car): Street Parking
Parking (Coach/Bus): As directed by Police
Other Clubs Sharing Ground: Sale Sharks RUFC
Police Force and Tel No: Greater Manchester (0161 872 5050)
Disabled Visitors' Facilities:
Wheelchairs: Main and Cheadle stands
Blind: Headsets available
Anticipated Development(s): Although the club is still planning for the reconstruction of the Railway End, with the intention of constructing a new 5,500-seat capacity stand on the site, there is no time scale for this work (which had originally been planned for 1999/2000). Theoretically, the next phase after the Railway End would be an upgrade to the Vernon BS Stand, with the intention of making the ground's capacity 20,000.

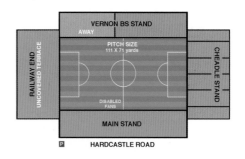

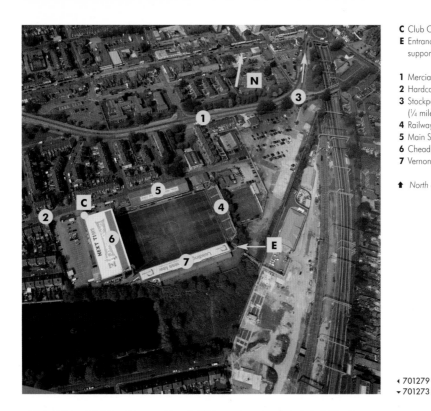

C Club Offices
E Entrance(s) for visiting
   supporters

1 Mercian Way
2 Hardcastle Road
3 Stockport BR station
   (¼ mile)
4 Railway End
5 Main Stand
6 Cheadle Stand
7 Vernon BS Stand

⬆ North direction (approx)

◀ 701279
▼ 701273

1 A50
2 To Stoke BR station
3 To A500 Queensway and
  City Centre, railway station
  and M6
4 North Stand
5 West Stand
6 East Stand
7 South Stand (away)
8 To Uttoxeter

↑ North direction (approx)

▸ 700729
▾ 700734

stoke city

Britannia Stadium, Stanley Matthews Way, Stoke-on-Trent, ST4 4EG

website: **WWW.STOKECITYFC.PREMIUMTV.CO.UK**
e:mail: **INFO@STOKECITYFC.COM**
tel no: **01782 592222**
colours: **RED AND WHITE STRIPED SHIRTS, WHITE SHORTS**
nickname: **THE POTTERS**
season 2008/09: **PREMIER LEAGUE**

During the 2007/08 season a number of clubs were vying for the automatic promotion places from the League Championship but it was relatively unfancied Stoke City under Tony Pulis that, towards the end of the season, seemed to have one of the two berths within the club's grasp. As with the other top teams, however, there was a distinct wobble in the team's form and it was not until the final day of the season that automatic promotion was achieved. Both Hull City and Stoke City could have claimed the final spot behind already promoted West Brom, but Hull's 1-0 defeat at Play-Off chasing Ipswich Town allied to Stoke's 0-0 draw with Leicester brings top-level football to Stoke City for the first time since 1985. The last time that Stoke were in the top division, the club was relegated with a then record low points total of 17; this dire record has now been well and truly smashed courtesy of both Sunderland and Derby County but the challenge for Pulis will be to strengthen the team sufficiently in the close season to avoid embarrassment this time round. As the gap between the established Premier League teams and those promoted gets ever greater, it's hard to escape the conclusion that City fans should enjoy the season as a one-off opportunity to visit grounds like Old Trafford and the Emirates as relegation is almost a certainty.

Advance Tickets Tel No: 0871 663 2008
Fax: 0871 663 2007
Training Ground: Michelin Sports Ground, Rose Tree Avenue, Trent Vale, Stoke On Trent, ST4 6NL
Brief History: Founded 1863 as Stoke F.C., amalgamated with Stoke Victoria in 1878, changed to Stoke City in 1925. Former Grounds: Sweetings Field, Victoria Ground (1878-1997), moved to new ground for start of 1997/98 season. Record attendance (at Victoria Ground): 51,380; at Britannia Stadium 28,218
(Total) Current Capacity: 28,383 (all seated)
Visiting Supporters' Allocation: 4,800 (in the South Stand)
Nearest Railway Station: Stoke-on-Trent
Parking (Car): The 650 parking spaces at the ground are for officials and guests only. The 1,600 spaces in the South car park are pre-booked only, with the majority held by season ticket holders. There is some on-street parking, but with a 10-15min walk.
Parking (Coach/Bus): As directed
Police Force and Tel No: Staffordshire (01782 744644)
Disabled Visitors' Facilities:
Wheelchairs: 164 places for disabled spectators
Blind: Commentaries available
Anticipated Development(s): There are long-term plans to increase the ground's capacity to 30,000 by the construction of a corner stand between the John Smith Stand and the Boothen End but there is no timescale for this work.

season 07/08: Championship **2ND** (promoted) p**46** w**21** d**16** l**9** gf**69** ga**55**

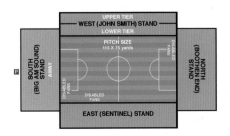

sunderland

Stadium of Light

website: **WWW.SAFC.COM**
e:mail: **ENQUIRIES@SAFC.COM**
tel no: **0191 551 5000**
colours: **RED AND WHITE STRIPED SHIRTS, BLACK SHORTS**
nickname: **THE BLACK CATS**
season 2008/09: **PREMIER LEAGUE**

Promoted at the end of the 2006/07 season, the new campaign was always going to be one of consolidation in the Premier League for Roy Keane's Black Cats and a position in 17th place or above was to be seen as a success. Throughout the season, although the relegation battle was always a bit too close for comfort, the club was always able to keep its head above the water. Ultimately finishing in 15th position three points above relegated Reading will undoubtedly be considered a triumph, particularly as both of the other promoted teams made an immediate return to the Championship, and with three potentially weaker teams being promoted in 2007/08, Sunderland ought to be able to make some progress in consolidating its Premier League status in the new season.

Advance Tickets Tel No: 0845 671 1973
Fax: 0191 551 5123
Training Ground: The Academy Of Light, Sunderland Road, Sunderland SR6 7UN
Brief History: Founded 1879 as 'Sunderland & District Teachers Association', changed to 'Sunderland Association' in 1880 and shortly after to 'Sunderland'. Former Grounds: Blue House Field, Groves Field (Ashbrooke), Horatio Street, Abbs Field, Newcastle Road and Roker Park (1898-1997); moved to Stadium of Light for the start of the 1997/98 season. Record crowd (at Roker Park): 75,118; at Stadium of Light (48,353)
(Total) Current Capacity: 49,000 (all seated)
Visiting Supporters' Allocation: 3,000 (South Stand)
Nearest Railway Station: Stadium of Light (Tyne & Wear Metro)
Parking (Car): Car park at ground reserved for season ticket holders. Limited on-street parking (but the police may decide to introduce restrictions). Otherwise off-street parking in city centre
Parking (Coach/Bus): As directed
Police Force and Tel No: Tyne & Wear (0191 510 2020)
Disabled Visitors' Facilities:
Wheelchairs: 180 spots
Blind: Commentary available
Anticipated Development(s): The club has planning permission to increase capacity at the Stadium of Light by 7,200 in an expanded Metro FM Stand and plans a further 9,000 in a second tier to the McEwans Stand, taking the ultimate capacity of the ground to 64,000. There is, however, no confirmed timescale.

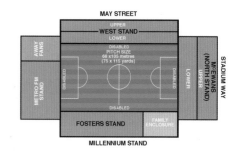

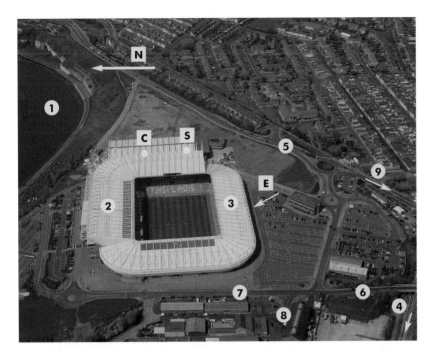

C Club Offices
S Club Shop
E Entrance(s) for visiting
   supporters

1 River Wear
2 North (McEwans) Stand
3 South (Metro FM) Stand
   (away)
4 To Sunderland BR station
   ($^1/_2$ mile)
5 Southwick Road
6 Stadium Way
7 Millennium Way
8 Hay Street
9 To Wearmouth Bridge (via
   A1018 North Bridge Street)
   to City Centre

↑ *North direction (approx)*

◄ 701290
▼ 701284

1 A4067 Ffordd Cwm Tawe Road
2 A4067 to A48 and M4 Junction 44 (five miles)
3 B4603 Neath Road
4 Brunel Way
5 Normandy Road
6 A4217
7 To Swansea city centre and BR railway station (two miles)
8 Parking
9 Cardiff-Swansea railway line

↑ North direction (approx)

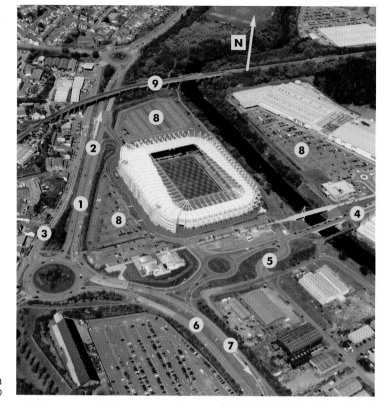

◄ 700168
▼ 700180

swansea city

Liberty Stadium, Morfa, Swansea SA1 2FA

website: **WWW.SWANSEACITY.PREMIUMTV.CO.UK**
e:mail: **INFO@SWANSEACITY.CO.UK**
tel no: **01792 616600**
colours: **WHITE SHIRTS, WHITE SHORTS**
nickname: **THE SWANS**
season2008/09: **CHAMPIONSHIP**

Under Roberto Martinez, Swansea City carried on where the team had left off in 2006/07 and were serious challengers for the Play-Offs and automatic promotion throughout the season and it came as little surprise that both promotion to the League Championship and the League One title were achieved well before the end of the campaign. Prolific up front and relatively mean in defence, the Swans had the best goal difference in the top two divisions of the Football League. There was, however, the occasional fly in the ointment, most notably an embarrassing 4-2 defeat away at non-League Havant & Waterlooville in the 3rd round of the FA Cup following an earlier draw at the Liberty Stadium. For the new season, Martinez will see the Swans play in English football's second tier for the first time in a number of years and the club will also be able to renew its local rivalry with Cardiff City. As a promoted team Swansea may take a time to establish themselves at the higher level but the club certainly has the potential to retain its new Championship status.

Telephone: 01792 616600
Advance Tickets Tel No: 0870 400004
Fax: 01792 616606
Training Ground: Llandarcy Academy of Sport, Neath SA10 6JD

Brief History: Founded 1900 as Swansea Town, changed to Swansea City in 1970. Former grounds: various, including Recreation Ground, and Vetch Field (1912-2005); moved to the new ground for the start of the 2005/06 season. Founder-members Third Division (1920). Record attendance (at Vetch Field): 32,796; (at Liberty Stadium) 19,288.
(Total) Current Capacity: 20,500 (all seated)
Visiting Supporters' Allocation: 3,500 maximum in North Stand
Nearest Railway Station: Swansea
Parking (Car): Adjacent to ground
Parking (Coach/Bus): As directed
Other Clubs Sharing Ground: Swansea Ospreys RUFC
Police Force and Tel No: South Wales (01792 456999)
Disabled Visitors' Facilities:
Wheelchairs: 252 spaces; *Blind:* No special facility
Anticipated Development(s): After several years of uncertainty, Swansea City relocated to the new White Rock Stadium with its 20,000 all-seater capacity for the start of the 2005/06 season. The ground, which cost £27 million to construct and which was built near the site of the old Morfa stadium, is shared by the Swansea Ospreys RUFC team.

season 07/08: League One **1ST** (promoted) p**46** w**27** d**11** l**8** gf**82** ga**42**

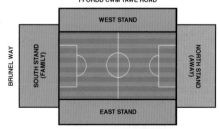

FFORDD CWM TAWE ROAD

WEST STAND

BRUNEL WAY

SOUTH STAND (FAMILY)

NORTH STAND (AWAY)

EAST STAND

swindon town

County Ground, County Road, Swindon, SN1 2ED

website: **WWW.SWINDONTOWNFC.PREMIUMTV.CO.UK**
e:mail: **ENQUIRIES@SWINDONTOWNFC.CO.UK**
tel no: **0871 423 6433**
colours: **RED SHIRTS, WHITE SHORTS**
nickname: **THE ROBINS**
season 2008/09: **LEAGUE ONE**

Promoted at the end of the 2006/07 season, the club's first aspiration under manager Paul Sturrock was to ensure League One survival. However, Sturrock's tenure at the County Ground was destined to be relatively short-lived as, in November following Ian Holloway's departure from Plymouth Argyle, Sturrock was allowed to rejoin a club that he had previously been manager of. The club appointed David Byrne as his successor; however, his reign was destined to be also relatively short-lived as, following a take-over of the club by Andrew Fitton in mid-January, Maurice Malpas was confirmed as the team's new manager. Under Malpas the club achieved a position of mid-table security. For 2008/09, having established themselves in League One, the Robins ought to be one of the teams looking to progress into the top half of the table.

Advance Tickets Tel No: 0871 223 2300
Fax: 01793 333703
Training Ground: Zurich, Wanborough, Swindon SN4 0DY
Brief History: Founded 1881. Former Grounds: Quarry Ground, Globe Road, Croft Ground, County Ground (adjacent to current Ground and now Cricket Ground), moved to current County Ground in 1896. Founder-members Third Division (1920). Record attendance 32,000
(Total) Current Capacity: 15,700 (all seated)
Visiting Supporters' Allocation: 3,342 (all seated) in Arkell's Stand and Stratton Bank (open)
Nearest Railway Station: Swindon
Parking (Car): Town Centre
Parking (Coach/Bus): Adjacent car park
Other Club Sharing Ground: Possibility of Bristol RUFC groundsharing if Memorial Ground rebuilt
Police Force and Tel No: Wiltshire (01793 528111)
Disabled Visitors' Facilities:
Wheelchairs: In front of Arkell's Stand
Blind: Commentary available
Anticipated Development(s): The proposed relocation to the west of the town, at Shaw Tip, was thwarted in July 2004 when the local council decided not to sacrifice the community forest located at the site. The failure of the proposed move, which had been opposed by residents and many fans, resulted in the club seeking planning permission to redevelop its existing ground in February 2005.

C Club Offices
S Club Shop
E Entrance(s) for visiting
supporters

1 Shrivenham Road
2 Stratton Bank (away)
3 A345 Queens Drive
 (M4 Junction 15 – 3½ miles)
4 Swindon BR Station
 (½ mile)
5 Town End
6 Car Park
7 County Cricket Ground
8 Nationwide Stand
9 Arkell's Stand
10 'Magic' Roundabout

↑ *North direction (approx)*

◄ 699231
▼ 699234

C Club Offices
S Club Shop
E Entrance(s) for visiting
   supporters

1 Park Lane
2 A1010 High Road
3 White Hart Lane BR station
4 Paxton Road
5 Worcester Avenue
6 West Stand
7 South Stand

⬆ *North direction (approx)*

▸ 700261
▾ 700254

tottenham hotspur

White Hart Lane, Bill Nicholson Way, 748 High Road, Tottenham, London N17 0AP

website: **WWW.TOTTENHAMHOTSPUR.COM**
e:mail: **EMAIL@TOTTENHAMHOTSPUR.COM**
tel no: **0844 499 5000**
colours: **WHITE SHIRTS, NAVY BLUE SHORTS**
nickname: **SPURS**
season2008/09: **PREMIER LEAGUE**

Despite being one of the bigger spenders during the close season, a poor start to the season at Spurs brought Martin Jol's regime into the spotlight. In perhaps one of the worst handled managerial departures of recent years, Jol was to be sacked on the same day as Spurs played a UEFA Cup match against Getafe. In one of the worst kept secrets (his name had been linked with the post almost from the start of the season), Juande Ramos — having resigned as boss at Sevilla — took over as the new manager at the end of October. Under Ramos the club's playing fortunes improved and a gradual climb up the Premier League table resulted, although the finishing position of 11th was considerably worse than that achieved in 2006/07. Away from the League, Ramos's first season also brought silverware to White Hart Lane for the first time since 1999 with victory over Chelsea in the final of the Carling Cup. This success ensures that UEFA Cup football will again be on offer in 2008/09. In terms of the new season much will depend upon the calibre of the squad that Ramos is able to develop at the club, particularly if, as seems likely, Dimitar Berbatov is one of many high-profile players to depart during the close season. The improvement in the team's performances after Ramos's appointment suggest that he has what it takes to develop Spurs into serious contenders for fourth or fifth place in the division, although it's hard to escape the conclusion that a top-three spot may be beyond the team's capabilities.

Ticket Line: 0844 499 5000
Fax: 020 8365 5005
Training Ground: Spurs Lodge, Luxborough Lane, Chigwell IG7 5AB
Brief History: Founded 1882 as 'Hotspur', changed name to Tottenham Hotspur in 1885. Former Grounds: Tottenham Marshes and Northumberland Park, moved to White Hart Lane in 1899. F.A. Cup winner 1901 (as a non-League club). Record attendance 75,038
(Total) Current Capacity: 36,257 (all seated)
Visiting Supporters' Allocation: 3,000 (in South and West Stands)
Nearest Railway Station: White Hart Lane plus Seven Sisters and Manor House (tube)
Parking (Car): Street parking (min ¼ mile from ground)
Parking (Coach/Bus): Northumberland Park coach park
Police Force and Tel No: Metropolitan (0208 801 3443)
Disabled Visitors' Facilities:
Wheelchairs: North and South Stands (by prior arrangement)
Blind: Commentary available
Anticipated Development(s): Original plans for the redevelopment of White Hart Lane into a 52,000-seat capacity ground, costing £300 million, have been scaled back and any work is now likely to feature an expanded East Stand for which planning permission has been granted by Haringay Council. Once completed this will see White Hart Lane's capacity approach 50,000 but there is no confirmed timescale for the work.

season 07/08: Premier League **11TH** p38 w11 d13 l14 gf66 ga61

HIGH ROAD (A1010)

WEST STAND
UPPER
LOWER
PITCH SIZE
110 X 73 yards
AWAY
PARK LANE
SOUTH STAND
UPPER
LOWER
DISABLED FANS
DISABLED FANS
NORTH STAND
UPPER
LOWER
PAXTON ROAD
LOWER
UPPER
EAST STAND
WORCESTER AVENUE

tranmere rovers

Prenton Park, Prenton Road West, Birkenhead, CH42 9PY

website: **WWW.TRANMEREROVERS.PREMIUMTV.CO.UK**
e:mail: **INFO@TRANMEREROVERS.CO.UK**
tel no: **0870 460 3333**
colours: **WHITE SHIRTS, WHITE SHORTS**
nickname: **ROVERS**
season 2008/09: **LEAGUE ONE**

Under Ronnie Moore, Rovers were amongst the teams vying for a Play-Off place for much of the season but were ultimately to finish in a disappointing 11th place — two places and two points worse than in 2006/07 — some 11 points off Southend in the all-important sixth place. Away from the League, the club suffered a 1-0 away defeat at Stockport County in the 1st round of the Carling Cup. For the new season Rovers should again feature in the battle to hit one of the Play-Off places but it's hard to see the club achieving much more than another top-half finish.

Tel No: 0870 460 3333
Advance Tickets Tel No: 0870 460 3332
Fax: 0151 609 0606
Training Ground: Raby Vale, Willaston Road, Clatterbridge CH63 4JG
Brief History: Founded 1884 as Belmont F.C., changed name to Tranmere Rovers in 1885 (not connected to earlier 'Tranmere Rovers'). Former grounds: Steele's Field and Ravenshaw's Field (also known as Old Prenton Park, ground of Tranmere Rugby Club), moved to (new) Prenton Park in 1911. Founder-members 3rd Division North (1921). Record attendance 24,424
(Total) Current Capacity: 16,587 (all seated)
Visiting Supporters' Allocation: 2,500 (all-seated) in Cow Shed Stand
Nearest Railway Station: Hamilton Square or Rock Ferry
Parking (Car): Car park at Ground
Parking (Coach/Bus): Car park at Ground
Police Force and Tel No: Merseyside (0151 709 6010)
Disabled Visitors' Facilities:
Wheelchairs: Main Stand
Blind: Commentary available

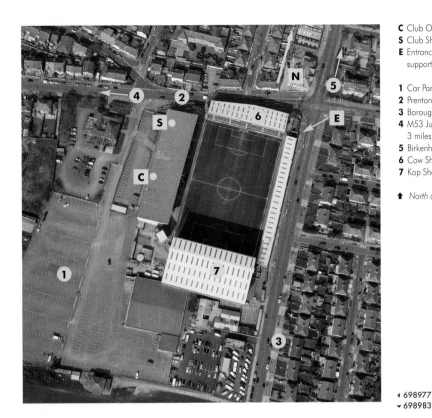

C Club Offices
S Club Shop
E Entrance(s) for visiting
   supporters

1 Car Park
2 Prenton Road West
3 Borough Road
4 M53 Junction 4 (B5151) –
   3 miles
5 Birkenhead (1 mile)
6 Cow Shed Stand
7 Kop Shed

↑ *North direction (approx)*

◄ 698977
▼ 698983

175

C Club Offices
S Club Shop
E Entrance(s) for visiting
   supporters

1 Motorway M6
2 M6 Junction 9
3 Bescot BR Station
4 Car Parks
5 Bescot Crescent
6 Gilbert Alsop Stand
7 William Sharp Stand

⬆ North direction (approx)

▶ 699950
▼ 699960

walsall

Banks's Stadium, Bescot Crescent, Walsall, West Midlands, WS1 4SA

website: **WWW.SADDLERS.PREMIUMTV.CO.UK**
e:mail: **INFO@WALSALLFC.CO.UK**
tel no: **0871 221 0442**
colours: **RED SHIRTS, RED SHORTS**
nickname: **THE SADDLERS**
season 2008/09: **LEAGUE ONE**

Promoted at the end of the 2007/08 season as League two champions following one season at the lower level, Walsall were one of the teams in the chasing pack for the Play-Offs in 2007/08. However, towards the end of the season, the Saddlers' form drifted away and the club slipped down to a position of mid-table security. Towards the end of the campaign, with the Play-Offs no longer a feasible possibility, Richard Money stood down as manager. New manager Jimmy Mullen (who had been appointed Money's assistant in the autumn of 2007), inherits a team that has proved itself at this higher level and the team should again be in a position to make a more concerted effort towards the Play-Offs.

Advance Tickets Tel No: 0871 663 0111/0222
Fax: 01922 613202
Training Ground: The Pavilion, Broad Lane, Essington, Wolverhampton WV11 2RH
Brief History: Founded 1888 as Walsall Town Swifts (amalgamation of Walsall Town – founded 1884 – and Walsall Swifts – founded 1885), changed name to Walsall in 1895. Former Grounds: The Chuckery, West Bromwich Road (twice), Hilary Street (later named Fellows Park, twice), moved to Bescot Stadium in 1990. Founder-members Second Division (1892). Record attendance 11,049 (25,453 at Fellows Park)
(Total) Current Capacity: 11,300 (all seated)
Visiting Supporters' Allocation: 2,000 maximum in William Sharp Stand
Nearest Railway Station: Bescot
Parking (Car): Car park at Ground
Parking (Coach/Bus): Car park at Ground
Police Force and Tel No: West Midlands (01922 638111)
Disabled Visitors' Facilities:
Wheelchairs: Bank's Stand *Blind*: No special facility
Anticipated Development(s): Planning permission was granted in the summer of 2004 for the redevelopment of the William Sharp Stand to add a further 2,300 seats, taking the away allocation up to 4,000 and the total ground capacity to 13,500. The project is to be funded via advertising directed towards the adjacent M6 but work has yet to commence.

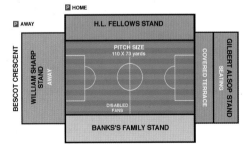

watford

Vicarage Road Stadium, Vicarage Road, Watford, WD18 0ER

website: **WWW.WATFORDFC.PREMIUMTV.CO.UK**
e:mail: **YOURVOICE@WATFORDFC.CO.UK**
tel no: **0845 442 1881**
colours: **YELLOW SHIRTS, RED SHORTS**
nickname: **THE HORNETS**
season 2008/09: **CHAMPIONSHIP**

season 07/08: Championship **6TH** p**46** w**18** d**12** l**12** gf**62** ga**56**

Relegated at the end of the 2006/07 season Adrian Boothroyd's Watford side was widely fancied to make an immediate return to the Premier League and early results seemed to suggest that automatic promotion was well within the team's capabilities. However, as the season wore on the Hornets' form slipped as did the team's position in the Championship with the result that the automatic promotion places disappeared and it was only results on the final day that kept the team in the Play-Off places. With Crystal Palace, Ipswich and Wolves all vying for the final two places, Watford's 1-1 draw at lowly Blackpool was sufficient, despite victories for both Ipswich and Wolves. Finishing in sixth place meant a Play-Off against Hull City and a 2-0 home defeat at Vicarage Road meant that Hull became favourites to make their first ever trip to Wembley. A 4-1 victory for the home side at the KC Stadium, making 6-1 on aggregate, means that Watford will face a second season back in the Championship. This will be the club's second season of parachute payments and probably represents a final opportunity to make a serious bid for a return to the Premier League as other ex-Premier League teams have tended to struggle once these payments have ended. However, with the three relegated teams from the Premier League looking to make an immediate return, the Hornets may well struggle to achieve anything more than a Play-Off place again.

Advance Tickets Tel No: 0845 442 1881
Fax: 01923 496001
Training Ground: University College London Sports Grounds, Bell Lane, London Colney, St Albans AL2 1BZ
Brief History: Founded 1898 as an amalgamation of West Herts (founded 1891) and Watford St. Mary's (founded early 1890s). Former Grounds: Wiggenhall Road (Watford St. Mary's) and West Herts Sports Ground, moved to Vicarage Road in 1922. Founder-members Third Division (1920). Record attendance 34,099
(Total) Current Capacity: 24,600 (all seated)
Visiting Supporters' Allocation: 4,500 maximum in Vicarage Road (North) Stand
Nearest Railway Station: Watford High Street or Watford Junction
Parking (Car): Nearby multi-storey car park in town centre (10 mins walk)
Parking (Coach/Bus): Cardiff Road car park
Other Clubs Sharing Ground: Saracens RUFC
Police Force and Tel No: Hertfordshire (01923 472000)
Disabled Visitors' Facilities:
Wheelchairs: Corner East Stand and South Stand (special enclosure for approx. 24 wheelchairs), plus enclosure in North East Corner
Blind: Commentary available in the East Stand (20 seats, free of charge)
Anticipated Development(s): It was announced in September 2006 that the club intended to undertake a £32 million redevelopment of Vicarage Road in conjunction with the housing association Origin. The scheme will see the construction of a new East Stand, taking the ground's capacity to almost 23,000, and is scheduled for completion in 2010. A planning application for the new East Stand was submitted in March 2008 with the hope that permission would be gained by the summer. The old stand will be demolished later in 2008.

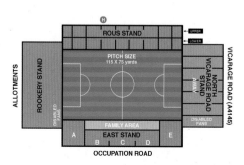

C Club Offices
S Club Shop

1 Vicarage Road
2 Occupation Road
3 Rous Stand
4 Town Centre (½ mile) – Car Parks, High Street BR Station
5 Vicarage Road Stand (away)
6 East Stand
7 Rookery End

⬆ *North direction (approx)*

◄ 701177
▼ 701188

C Club Offices
S Club Shop
E Entrance(s) for visiting
   supporters

1 A41 Birmingham Road
2 To M5 Junction 1
3 Birmingham Centre
   (4 miles)
4 Halfords Lane
5 Main Stand
6 Smethwick End
7 Rolfe Street, Smethwick BR
   Station (1½ miles)
8 To The Hawthorns BR Station
9 East (Rainbow) Stand
10 Apollo 2000 Stand

↑ North direction (approx)

▶ 701132
▼ 701130

west bromwich albion

The Hawthorns, Halfords Lane, West Bromwich, West Midlands B71 4LF

website: **WWW.WBA.PREMIUMTV.CO.UK**
e:mail: **ENQUIRIES@WBAFC.CO.UK**
tel no: **0871 271 1100**
colours: **NAVY BLUE AND WHITE STRIPED SHIRTS, WHITE SHORTS**
nickname: **THE BAGGIES**
season 2008/09: **FA PREMIERSHIP**

Although the League Championship was the division from which nobody seemed to be able to make a sustained bid for promotion — a number of teams held places in the top two at various stages during the campaign before being sucked back into the pack — West Brom were there or thereabouts all season and ultimately the club regained its Premier League spot and the Championship title. Stoke ultimately became the club's only opposition to the title and results on the final day — Stoke's 0-0 draw with Leicester City and the Baggies' 2-0 victory at QPR — ensured that the title passed to the Hawthorns. With a goals for total of 88, West Brom were the most prolific scorers in all four divisions, although the club also conceded 55 league goals (10 more than relegated Leicester). Away from the League, the club also had a successful FA Cup campaign before losing to Portsmouth in a closely fought semi-final at Wembley. For 2008/09 Tony Mowbray will undoubtedly have to strengthen his squad if the Baggies are not to make an immediate return to the League Championship. Of the three teams that went up in 2006/07, two made an immediate return and fans will be hoping that West Brom can emulate Sunderland rather than Birmingham City but it will be a close call.

Advance Tickets Tel No: 0871 271 9780
Fax: 0871 271 9861
Training Ground: Halfords Lane, West Bromwich B71 4LQ (the team also occasionally trains at the University of Aston ground at Great Barr)
Brief History: Founded 1879. Former Grounds: Coopers Hill, Dartmouth Park, Four Acres, Stoney Lane, moved to the Hawthorns in 1900. Founder-members of Football League (1888). Record attendance 64,815
(Total) Current Capacity: 28,000 (all seated)
Visiting Supporters' Allocation: 3,000 in Smethwick End (can be increased to 5,200 if required)
Nearest Railway Station: The Hawthorns
Parking (Car): Halfords Lane and Rainbow Stand car parks
Parking (Coach/Bus): Rainbow Stand car park
Police Force and Tel No: West Midlands (0121 554 3414)
Disabled Visitors' Facilities:
Wheelchairs: Apollo 2000 and Smethwick Road End
Blind: Facility available
Anticipated Development(s): There is speculation that the club will seek to increase capacity to 30,000 by rebuilding the area between the Apollo and East stands, but nothing is confirmed.

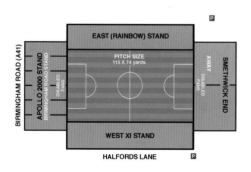

west ham united

Boleyn Ground, Green Street, Upton Park, London, E13 9AZ

website: **WWW.WHUFC.CO.UK**
e:mail: **YOURCOMMENTS@WESTHAMUNITED.CO.UK**
tel no: **020 854**
colours: **CLARET AND BLUE SHIRTS, WHITE SHORTS**
nickname: **THE HAMMERS**
season 2008/09: **PREMIER LEAGUE**

season 07/08: Premier League **10TH** p**38** w**13** d**10** l**15** gf**42** ga**50**

Following the drama of the 2006/07 season, when the Hammers retained their Premier League status in somewhat controversial circumstances, the 2007/08 season proved to be significantly less fraught for the Upton Park faithful. Under Alan Curbishley the team was secure in a mid-table position although, whilst effective, the manager's style of play did not find universal favour amongst the fans. Finishing in 10th place was a distinct improvement on 2006/07 although it's hard to escape the conclusion that, outside the top four or five and the bottom three or four, the Premier League is composed of relatively ordinary teams and a few good or bad results can have a dramatic impact on the club's ultimate position. One interesting fact to emerge at the end of the season was that, of all the Premier League teams, West Ham's starting 11 included more English-qualified players on average (6.6 per game) than any other team. Contrast this with Arsenal (where an English-qualified player started, on average, one League game in three). For 2008/09, it's likely that the Hammers will again be one of those teams that feature in a position of mid-table anonymity: too good to be involved in the relegation battle, particularly given the three teams being promoted, but not strong enough to sustain a serious challenge to the top six. Moreover, it's also hard to escape the conclusion that, without a dramatic improvement in the team's style of play, Curbishley's position will become more tenuous as fans become increasingly alienated.

Advance Tickets Tel No: 0870 112 2700
Fax: 020 8548 2758
Training Ground: Chadwell Heath, Saville Road, Romford RM6 6DT
Brief History: Founded 1895 as Thames Ironworks, changed name to West Ham United in 1900. Former Grounds: Hermit Road, Browning Road, The Memorial Ground, moved to Boleyn Ground in 1904. Record attendance 42,322
(Total) Current Capacity: 35,146 (all seated)
Visiting Supporters' Allocation: 3,600 maximum
Nearest Railway Station: Barking BR, Upton Park (tube)
Parking (Car): Street parking
Parking (Coach/Bus): As directed by Police
Police Force and Tel No: Metropolitan (020 8593 8232)
Disabled Visitors' Facilities:
Wheelchairs: West Lower, Bobby Moore and Centenary Stands
Blind: Commentaries available
Anticipated Development(s): The idea that West Ham United might take over the 2012 Olympic Stadium was quashed in the spring of 2007. The club's new Icelandic owners have, however, decided to examine the possibility of relocation to a new 50,000-seat ground on a former Parcelforce site in east London although nothing is confirmed at this stage.

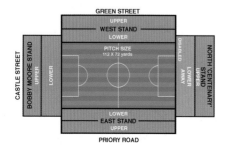

E Entrance(s) for visiting
supporters

1 A124 Barking Road
2 Green Street
3 North Stand
4 Upton Park Tube Station
(¼ mile)
5 Barking BR Station (1 mile)
6 Bobby Moore Stand
7 East Stand
8 West Stand

⬆ *North direction (approx)*

◄ 701322
▼ 701332

C Club Offices
E Entrance(s) for visiting
   supporters

1 Loire Drive
2 Anjoy Boulevard
3 Car Parks
4 Robin Park Arena
5 River Douglas
6 Leeds-Liverpool Canal
7 To A577/A49 and Wigan
   town centre plus Wigan
   (Wallgate) and Wigan
   (North Western) station
8 East Stand
9 South Stand
10 North Stand
11 West Stand

↑ North direction (approx)

▶ 701090
▼ 701097

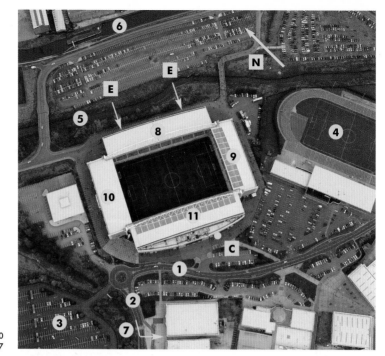

wigan athletic

JJB Stadium, Robin Park Complex, Newtown, Wigan, Lancashire, WN5 0UZ

website: **WWW.WIGANLATICS.PREMIUMTV.CO.UK**
e:mail: **S.HAYTON@JJBSTADIUM.CO.UK**
tel no: **01942 774000**
colours: **WHITE AND BLUE SHIRTS, BLUE SHORTS**
nickname: **THE LATICS**
season 2008/09: **PREMIER LEAGUE**

Widely tipped as being likely to be the first Premier League managerial casualty, Chris Hutchings actually managed to outlast both Jose Mourinho and Martin Jol before the axeman came calling in early November with the Latics now rooted in the Premier League's drop zone. Ironically, Hutchings lasted exactly the same number of League games — 12 — as he achieved during his previous managerial spell at Bradford City in the Premier League. A reasonably bright start to the season was derailed as a result of injuries to key players, most notably Emile Heskey, and Hutchings departed after the 2-0 home defeat to Chelsea. Frank Barlow took over as caretaker whilst chairman Dave Whelan sought a replacement. Whilst ex-boss Paul Jewell was rumoured to be in the frame for a rapid return to the JJB Stadium, this was soon ruled out and the club made a move for Birmingham boss Steve Bruce, who thus returned to Athletic for his second spell in charge. Under Bruce, Wigan secured their Premier League status with a 2-0 away victory at high-flying Aston Villa in the penultimate game of the season and could thus go into the last game — the trifling affair of a home match against title-chasing Manchester United — confident that whatever the result, Wigan would remain in the top flight for a further season. Provided that Wigan avoid the injuries that plagued the start of the 2007/08 season and that the players brought in by Bruce remain for the new season, Latics' fans should be reasonably confident that the 2008/09 campaign should see the club again retain Premier league status, particularly given the relative weakness of the promoted teams although the fact that the club was the lowest scoring team outside Derby in the division may be a cause for concern.

Advance Tickets Tel No: 0871 663 3552
Fax: 01942 770477
Training Ground: Christopher Park, Wigan Lower Road, Standish Lower Ground, Wigan WN6 8LB
Brief History: Founded 1932. Springfield Park used by former Wigan Borough (Football League 1921-1931) but unrelated to current club. Elected to Football League in 1978 (the last club to be elected rather than promoted). Moved to JJB Stadium for start of 1999/2000 season. Record attendance at Springfield Park 27,500; at JJB Stadium 25,023
(Total) Current Capacity: 25,000 (all seated)
Visiting Supporters' Allocation: 5,400 (maximum) in North Stand (all-seated)
Nearest Railway Stations: Wigan Wallgate/Wigan North Western (both about 1.5 miles away)
Parking (Car): 2,500 spaces at the ground
Parking (Coach/Bus): As directed
Other Clubs Sharing Ground: Wigan Warriors RLFC
Police Force and Tel No: Greater Manchester (0161 872 5050)
Disabled Visitors' Facilities:
Wheelchairs: 100 spaces; *Blind*: No special facility although it is hoped to have a system in place shortly
Anticipated Development(s): None following completion of the ground.

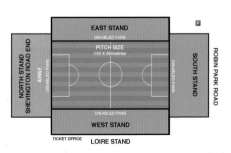

wolverhampton wanderers

Molineux Ground, Waterloo Road, Wolverhampton, WV1 4QR

website: **WWW.WOLVES.PREMIUMTV.CO.UK**
e:mail: **INFO@WOLVES.CO.UK**
tel no: **0870 442 0123**
colours: **GOLD SHIRTS, BLACK SHORTS**
nickname: **WOLVES**
season 2008/09: **CHAMPIONSHIP**

Never quite strong enough to make a push for the automatic promotion places, Mick McCarthy's Wolves side were, however, in the hunt for a Play-Off place right through until the final Sunday of the season. Needing a good result against Plymouth, Wolves needed results elsewhere — most notably at Blackpool, where Watford were playing, and Crystal Palace, where Burnley were the visitors — to sneak into the top six. In the event, results elsewhere meant that Wolves' 1-0 victory was rendered irrelevant and thus Wolves will face a further season in the Championship in 2008/09. The club also struggled in the Carling Cup, losing 3-1 to League Two newcomers Morecambe in the 2nd round. It's hard to escape the conclusion that Wolves will again face an uphill task to reach even the Play-Offs and, if the season starts poorly, the fans' increasing displeasure over McCarthy's regime may well put the manager's position at risk.

Advance Tickets Tel No: 0870 442 0123
Fax: 01902 687006
Training Ground: The Sir Jack Hayward Training Ground, Douglas Turner Way, Wolverhampton WV3 9BF
Brief History: Founded 1877 as St. Lukes, combined with Goldthorn Hill to become Wolverhampton Wanderers in 1884. Former Grounds: Old Windmill Field, John Harper's Field and Dudley Road, moved to Molineux in 1889. Founder-members Football League (1888). Record attendance 61,315
(Total) Current Capacity: 28,500 (all seated)
Visiting Supporters' Allocation: 3,200 in lower tier of Steve Bull Stand or 2,000 in Jack Harris Stand
Nearest Railway Station: Wolverhampton
Parking (Car): West Park and adjacent North Bank
Parking (Coach/Bus): As directed by Police
Police Force and Tel No: West Midlands (01902 649000)
Disabled Visitors' Facilities:
Wheelchairs: 104 places on two sides
Blind: Commentary (by prior arrangement)
Anticipated Developments: The club installed some 900 seats on a temporary stand – now removed – between the Billy Wright and Jack Harris stands for the season in the Premiership. The club has plans to expand the capacity of Molineux to more than 40,000 by adding second tiers to the Stan Cullis and Jack Harris stands and completely rebuilding the Steve Bull Stand. There is no timescale for the work but it is unlikely to proceed until the club regains (and retains) a place in the Premiership.

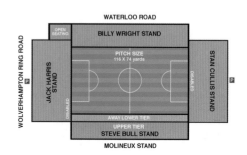

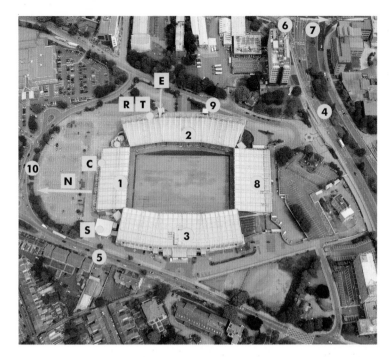

C Club Offices
S Club Shop
E Entrance(s) for visiting
   supporters
R Refreshment bars for visiting
   supporters
T Toilets for visiting supporters

1 Stan Cullis Stand
2 Steve Bull Stand
3 Billy Wright Stand
4 Ring Road – St. Peters
5 Waterloo Road
6 A449 Stafford Street
7 BR Station (½ mile)
8 Jack Harris Stand
9 Molineux Street
10 Molineux Way

↑ *North direction (approx)*

◀ 700864
▼ 700855

C Club Offices
S Club Shop
E Entrance(s) for visiting
  supporters

1 Car Park
2 Hillbottom Road
  (Industrial Estate)
3 M40 Junction 4
  (approx 2 miles)
4 Wycombe Town Centre
  (approx 2½ miles)
5 Woodlands Stand
6 Dreams Stand (away)
7 Syan Stand
8 Amersham & Wycombe
  College Stand

⬆ North direction (approx)

▶ 701154
▼ 701160

wycombe wanderers

Adams Park, Hillbottom Road, Sands, High Wycombe, Bucks HP12 4HU

website: **WWW.WYCOMBEWANDERERS.PREMIUMTV.CO.UK**
e:mail: **WWFC@WWFC.COM**
tel no: **01494 472 100**
colours: **SKY BLUE WITH NAVY BLUE QUARTERED SHIRTS, BLUE SHORTS**
nickname: **THE CHAIRBOYS**
season 2008/09: **LEAGUE TWO**

A season of some success at Wycombe saw Paul Lambert's side improve on the 2006/07 season and ultimately finish in seventh place thereby securing a Play-Off place. However, a 1-1 draw at home coupled with a 1-0 defeat away means the Chairboys face another season in League Two. After the defeat in the Play-Off semi-final, Paul Lambert announced that he was considering his position and he stood down shortly thereafter. The club moved swiftly in appointing the experienced Peter Taylor to the vacant position and he inherits a team that should once again be capable of reaching the Play-Offs at the very least.

Advance Tickets Tel No: 01494 441118
Fax: 01494 527633
Training Ground: Marlow Road, Marlow, SL7 3DQ
Brief History: Founded 1884. Former Grounds: The Rye, Spring Meadows, Loakes Park, moved to Adams Park 1990. Promoted to Football League 1993. Record attendance 15,678 (Loakes Park); 10,000 (Adams Park)
(Total) Current Capacity: 10,000 (8,250 seated)
Visiting Supporters' Allocation: c2,000 in the Dreams (ex-Roger Vere) Stand
Nearest Railway Station: High Wycombe (2½ miles)
Parking (Car): At Ground and Street parking
Parking (Coach/Bus): At Ground
Other Clubs Sharing Ground: London Wasps RUFC
Police Force and Tel No: Thames Valley (01494 465888)
Disabled Visitors' Facilities:
Wheelchairs: Special shelter – Main Stand, Hillbottom Road end; *Blind*: Commentary available
Anticipated Development(s): The club is examining its options with a view to a possible relocation to a new 15,000-capacity stadium adjacent to Junction 4 of the M40 although nothing is confirmed at this stage.

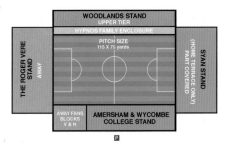

yeovil town

Huish Park, Lufton Way, Yeovil, Somerset, BA22 8YF

website: **WWW.YTFC.PREMIUMTV.CO.UK**
e:mail: **YTFC@YTFC.CO.UK**
tel no: **01935 423662**
colours: **GREEN SHIRTS, WHITE SHORTS**
nickname: **THE GLOVERS**
season 2008/09: **LEAGUE ONE**

Having made the Play-Offs at the end of the 2006/07 season, there were high hopes at Huish Park that Russell Slade's team could again mount a serious push towards the Play-Offs again in 2007/08. In the event, however, Yeovil were slightly more concerned about events at the other end of the table. Never seriously in the real battle for relegation, finishing in 18th place only two points above relegated Bournemouth is, however, a harsh reality check. Away from the League, the club's tradition of giant-killing acts was reversed in the Carling and FA cups, with the team losing to lower league opposition in both: 4-1 at League Two Hereford United in the first round of the former and 4-1 away at Blue Star Premier Torquay United in the latter. The team's fundamental problem was in front of goal and a League total of 38 was by far the worst in League One. With several highly ambitious and well-funded teams coming up in 2008/09 and with no guarantee that other relegation candidates will give their opponents an advantage by entering Administration this time round, Yeovil could well struggle to retain the club's current status unless Slade can recruit more firepower up front.

Advance Tickets Tel No: 01935 423662
Fax: 01935 473956
Training Ground: Huish Park (see above); the club has plans to relocate these facilities to Kingsbury Episcopi
Brief History: Founded as Yeovil Casuals in 1895 and merged with Petters United in 1920. Moved to old ground (Huish) in 1920 and relocated to Huish Park in 1990. Founder members of Alliance Premier League in 1979 but relegated in 1985. Returned to Premier League in 1988 but again relegated in 1996. Promoted to the now retitled Conference in 1997 and promoted to the Nationwide League in 2003. Record Attendance: (at Huish) 16,318 (at Huish Park) 9,348
(Total) Current Capacity: 9,400 (5,212 seated)
Visiting Supporters' Allocation: 1,700 on Copse Road Terrace (open) plus Limited seats in the Main Stand.
Nearest Railway Station: Yeovil Junction or Yeovil Pen Mill
Parking (Car): Car park near to stadium for 800 cars
Parking (Coach/Bus): As directed
Police Force and Tel No: Avon & Somerset (01935 415291)
Disabled Visitors' Facilities:
Wheelchairs: Up to 20 dedicated located in the Bartlett Stand
Blind: No special facility

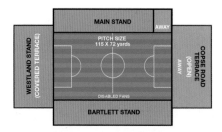

1 Western Avenue
2 Copse Road
3 Lufton Way
4 Artillery Road
5 Main (Yeovil College) Stand
6 Bartlett Stand
7 Westland Stand
8 Copse Road Terrace (away)
9 Memorial Road
10 Mead Avenue
11 To town centre (one mile) and
   stations (two to four miles)

↑ North direction (approx)

◄ 700937
▼ 700947

millennium stadium

Westgate Street, Cardiff, CF10 1JA

website: **WWW.MILLENNIUMSTADIUM.COM**
e:mail: **INFO@CARDIFF-STADIUM.CO.UK**
tel no: **0870 0138600**
Fax: **029 2023 2678**
Stadium Tours: **029 208 22228**

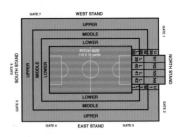

Brief History: The stadium, built upon the site of the much-loved and historic Cardiff Arms Park, was opened in 2000 and cost in excess of £100 million (a tiny sum in comparison with the current forecast spend of over £600 million on the redevelopment of Wembley). As the national stadium for Wales, the ground will be primarily used in sporting terms by Rugby Union, but was used by the FA to host major fixtures (such as FA Cup and Carling Cup finals) until 2007 when the new Wembley was completed.

(Total) Current Capacity: 72,500 (All seated)
Nearest Railway Station: Cardiff Central
Parking (Car): Street parking only.
Parking (Coach/Bus): As directed by the police
Police Force and Tel No: South Wales (029 2022 2111)
Disabled Visitors' Facilities:
Wheelchairs: c250 designated seats. The whole stadium has been designed for ease of disabled access with lifts, etc.
Blind: Commentary available.
Anticipated Development(s): None planned